THE DISCIPLINED LIFE

The Disciplined Life

by

Richard Shelley Taylor

Discipline must ever precede liberty
—H. ORTON WILEY

BEACON HILL PRESS
OF KANSAS CITY

ISBN 978-0-8341-0272-9

LIBRARY OF CONGRESS NO. 62-7123

Printed in the United States of America

40   39   38   37   36

Dedicated to

AMY

—whose example of disciplined living
has been an unfailing inspiration during the years of our happy pilgrimage
together.

Acknowledgments

The following publishers have kindly granted permission to quote from their publications:

Ginn and Company, Boston, Massachusetts: *The Problem of Choice*, William Henry Roberts.

Macmillan Company, New York, New York: *Fritz Kreisler*, Louis P. Lochner.

Thomas Nelson & Sons, New York, New York: *Revised Standard Version of the Holy Bible*, copyrighted 1946 and 1952 by the Division of Christian Education of the National Council of Churches.

New Zealand Herald, Auckland, New Zealand. Quotation from leading article.

Fleming H. Revell Company, Westwood, New Jersey: *The Minister's Obstacle*, Ralph G. Turnbull.

Saturday Evening Post, Philadelphia, Pennsylvania: Editorial, Dr. Harry A. Snyder, December 3, 1960.

Dr. Benjamin Spock, *Baby and Child Care*. The author is especially grateful to Dr. Spock for a personal letter in which he explained some of the changes in the revised edition of his famous book, *Baby and Child Care*, and for permission to quote this letter.

Contents

Foreword

"God will not look you over for medals—but for scars" (Hubbard). That is another way of saying He wants no "pampered saints." In today's turbulent world God needs disciplined men—soldiers tried, true, and battle-ready!

The plight of modern man may be summed up in his striving for the road of self-indulgence. The way of least resistance is his goal. Sacrifice, discipline, restraint—these words present "ideas" that are hard to come by in our generation.

With bold, deft strokes from his ready pen, Dr. Richard S. Taylor penetrates the shallowness of our culture and lays bare the dire need for disciplined living. The truth is we are living in an age wired for sound, but the sounds are ominous.

Dr. Taylor writes well. More important still, the writing comes from a full heart, a well-furnished mind, and a life dedicated to do the will of God. He sees the perils of modern society and shows us how to avoid them.

I commend the reading of *The Disciplined Life* to all persons who in an age of weakness would remain strong, in a time of confusion would retain their sense of direction, and in a period of humanism and doubt would cling to those imperishable values of the Spirit.

—S. T. Ludwig

Introduction

Discipline is what moderns need the most and want the least.

Too often young people who leave home, students who quit school, husbands and wives who seek divorce, church members who neglect services, employees who walk out on their jobs are simply trying to escape discipline. The true motive may often be camouflaged by a hundred excuses, but behind the flimsy front is the hard core of aversion to restraint and control.

Much of our restlessness and instability can be traced to this basic fault in modern character. Our overflowing asylums and hospitals and jails are but symptoms of an undisciplined age. There may be many secondary causes and there may be many secondary cures, but somewhere behind them all is the need for discipline. The kind of discipline needed is far deeper than the rule of alarm clocks and time cards; it embraces self-restraint, courage, perseverance, and resiliency as the inner panoply of the soul.

Many nervous and emotional disorders are the accumulated result of years of self-indulgent living. I am not thinking of the drunkards or the libertines, but of the respectable Christians who probably would be horrified at the thought of touching liquor or of indulging in gross immorality. But they are nevertheless undisciplined, and the fatal weakness is unmasked in the day of trial and adversity. A lifelong pattern of running away from difficulties, of avoiding incompatible people, of seeking the easy way, of quitting when the going gets rough finally shows up in neurotic semi-invalidism and incapacity. Numerous books may be read, many doctors and preachers consulted, innumerable prayers may be offered, and religious commitments made; the patient may be inundated with drugs, advice, costly treatment, and spiritual scourgings; yet none lay bare the real cause: lack of discipline. And the only real cure is to become a disciplined person.

The Bible says, "If thou faint in the day of adversity, thy strength is small." Days of adversity are bound to come. The weakling will faint by self-induced illness, by blaming others, by resigning, by displays of "nerves"— almost any method which presents the possibility of escape. Only by consistent disciplined living can that strength of character be developed which can face adversities without fainting.

The flood of moral looseness which, in this generation, has so blighted our youth and undermined our homes is in my opinion directly related to the self-indulgence of the age. And the Church has not escaped. The easy style of living and spending of these years of plenty has seeped into Christian circles too, even into our parsonages. As a result we have a lot of flabby saints and playboy preachers. We have given lip service to the altar of the Lord but in practice have bowed at the shrine of the swank. We have been mesmerized by materialism ourselves even while protesting against it in others. We have been thrown off balance by the prevailing false standards of value.

The remedy is not poverty and economic depression, but discipline. Christians in a land of bulging supermarkets must discipline their appetites lest they fatten their bodies and stupefy their souls by habitual gormandizing. They must beware the subtle, insidious tendency to judge the importance of themselves and others by the flashiness of their cars and the cut of their clothes. They must cease from careless spending and showy extravagance, not on the grounds of being unable to afford it, but on the grounds of principle. The alarming tide of moral casualties of recent years in both pulpit and pew is without question the result of that inner softness born of undisciplined, self-indulgent living. As Jack Ford says, "It is either discipline or decadence."

It is easy for some of us to say glibly that all that is needed is a genuine experience of entire sanctification. The true relationship of holiness to discipline is discussed in this volume, so need not be previewed here in detail. But we can anticipate by replying that the truth or falsity of the claim is in the word "genuine." Our people too often get an emotional experience of "sanctification" which is totally unrelated in their thinking to any form of rugged self-denial. They are not apt to obtain *genuine* holiness of heart unless they see clearly in advance that holiness both implies and demands discipline, in all of its forms and facets and at all levels of daily living.

If this book can in any measure put iron into our souls by promoting disciplined living, then its ministry will be timely indeed. And in all candor this too may be said: If the reader of the book is helped half as much by the reading as the writer has been by the writing, its publication will be abundantly justified.

RICHARD S. TAYLOR

PART ONE
The Place of Discipline in Christian Living

CHAPTER ONE

Discipline the Key to Power

National Power

The world belongs to the disciplined. One of the most ominous disclosures which has come out of Russia in recent years is the revelation that Communist youth are subjected to a far more intensive and exacting training than most young people in the Western nations. The American way of life, on the other hand, accents relaxation and recreation. It is true, we talk about American high pressure and the fast American pace, which is sending so many to mental hospitals, but this is the fast pace, not of the disciplined, but of the undisciplined. It is energetic striving, not for self-improvement, but for a good time. The American works feverishly to get ahead materially, but in it all he is determined to have his pleasures. He wants to eat his cake and have it too. Therefore the assertion that the American accent is on recreation and relaxation is supportable in spite of the paradoxical tension.

The Western world loves to play. Up to a point this is good. But when play—whether vicarious play via TV or grandstand, or play via personal participation—consumes a larger proportion of leisure time, money, conversation, and interest than is warranted by its cultural and recreative returns, then the play becomes the mark of a decadent age and the badge of softness rather than strength. It takes discipline to learn a new art, or science, or skill; it takes no discipline to watch a ball game or a wrestling match.

There was a time when intercollegiate debating drew big crowds. Now the debates are held in side rooms, while the crowd cheers at the basketball game. This shift of interest from the intellectual to the recreational has occurred even in Christian colleges—so widespread is the accent on relaxation and recreation. It must be emphatically asserted that the shift of excited popular interest from debates to basketball is a sign of cultural decline.

True enough, some discipline is involved in athletic training. But the discipline of the mind is on a higher level. Apart from divine intervention, the nation which produces the most scientists and educators will dominate the world, not the nation that produces the best sportsmen. Today the Russian scientists are seriously threatening American supremacy in industrial technology, mass production, military might, and space conquest. Which is more vital to the welfare of the world—the discipline that wins golden eagles at the Olympics or the discipline that outstrips the world on economic, military, and political levels?

Immediately following World War II the American GI in Europe earned a reputation for being "kindhearted but undisciplined." Kindheartedness is a virtue when coupled with moral stability. Without discipline kindheartedness becomes sentimental weakness. No nation has survived which has become self-indulgent and flabby. There is no reason to hope that Western nations which discard disciplined living will prove an exception. If communism finally conquers the world, it will not be because of better ideology, but because of better discipline.

Communist Lenin once said: "With a handful of dedicated people who will give me their lives, I will control the world." Let us compare this with the warning of Theodore Roosevelt: "The things that will destroy America are prosperity at any price, peace at any price, safety first instead of duty first, the love of soft living, and the get rich theory of life."[1] Will our aversion to discipline be the Achilles' heel which will turn Roosevelt's warning into prophecy and Lenin's boast into fact?

Personal Power

Not only nationally and politically, but in every realm, the race belongs to the disciplined. In the battle of ideas the disciplined mind has the advantage over the scatterbrain. A trained mind can evaluate evidence, think logically, select ends, and devise means; it can concentrate on essentials and discard the irrelevant. A trained mind can think more rapidly and also more accurately. At the same time the man with the ready mind is more apt to express himself coherently and persuasively. Consequently the man whose mind is undisciplined will soon be outclassed and outdistanced by others in whatever field he enters. He will find himself not only on a lower scale economically, but dominated socially by those who are more efficient. The peril is that the social subordination may become political subjugation. Master minds know how to manipulate the unthinking masses to the perpetuation of their own power. The undisciplined mind is always an easy prey for the demagogue and the charlatan. Out of such mass intellectual dullness and inertia dictatorships are spawned.

Although the discipline of the body is of less importance, it can be indispensable to power if its object is to train the body to serve the mind in the attaining of worthy objectives. The ability of Thomas Edison to sleep and awaken at will and to work through grueling, unbroken stretches, undoubtedly contributed to his greatness as an inventor. In April, 1941, Fritz Kreisler was forced by his accident to lay aside his violin for many

[1]Quoted by Charles Nutter in *Vital Speeches of the Day*, March 1, 1961.

weeks. When finally he tuned his instrument once again, his fingers were so stiff that playing seemed impossible. "But my desire was so intense," he reported later, "and I told myself: These are my fingers. These are my slaves. I am the general. I order them to play and I will them to action.

"You know—they played."[2]

The discipline of the years had carried over.

The advantage of the man with the disciplined body is most apt to be seen in his superior health and longevity. His better health will give him greater efficiency and effectiveness, while added years will extend his fruitfulness and power. Undisciplined living from twenty years of age to fifty is not likely to result in undiminished powers at seventy.

The fact that Moses reached the age of one hundred twenty years with his natural vitality unabated may have been due partially to the forty years in the wilderness as a shepherd, when his body became inured to summer heat and winter frost. We do know that John Wesley ascribed his preservation to his practice of rising at four o'clock and preaching at five. Though such a routine would shorten rather than extend the life of some men, particularly in this age of late nights—and disciplined *avoidance* of that kind of "Wesleyanism" might be wiser —it is still true that the man who learns to "keep his body under" is more likely to avoid being not only a castaway spiritually but a castaway physically.

We have talked about a disciplined mind and a disciplined body. Actually, of course, these are but adjuncts of a disciplined character. This is the great lack, the fatal deficiency. Too many of us are weak as persons. There may be an outstanding strong ability which has been cultivated by an intense training within that narrow sphere, such as a steady hand and keen eye in playing

[2]Louis P. Lochner, *Fritz Kreisler*, p. 88.

golf, without general strength of character.   But if one is weak as a person, the specialized ability will be progressively choked by the growth of vices until it will be lost.   A physician of my acquaintance had outstanding talents, but his indulgence in drink and immorality first cost him his reputation, then his practice, then his life—and certainly his soul.   The professional discipline represented by years of arduous study in medical school was finally dissolved in the larger weakness of character.

When Personal Power Tells

The superior power and efficiency of disciplined character are seen especially in great crises, times of sickness or bereavement, or financial adversity.   A woman in Boston approached the very brink of nervous collapse through strain and overwork.   She was unable to sleep, and was tortured with the sensation of crawling things on her skin, which gave rise to an almost irresistible urge to claw at her own flesh.   When she was hospitalized, the doctor told her frankly that, whatever drugs might be given, the conquest of the condition depended on her mental self-control, and her ability to refrain from scratching.   Years of discipline came to her rescue.   She lay quietly, holding her arms by her side, when her whole nervous system wanted to scream and writhe.   After a few days the condition subsided and the recuperative powers of enforced rest soon sent her home a well woman.

The discipline of mind and body which was demanded was made possible by years of habitual self-control and intelligent direction in her total life.   Disciplined character paid dividends.   Weak character would have succumbed to the imperious clamoring of the nervous system, and a long and tragic mental break would have been the result.   This is not to imply that prolonged physical or mental illness is always a proof of weak character, but it does suggest that in many cases such complete breakdowns could be prevented if there were the background of disciplined character to handle the situation wisely and in time.

Too often modern doctors practice in weak concession to the spineless self-indulgence of modern character, by avoiding those methods which impose self-discipline on the patient. It is easier to prescribe the things they know the patient would like to do, such as "taking it easier," or taking sweet-tasting nostrums, or maybe going on a trip, when possibly down in their hearts they know that none of these palliatives touch the real need.

Disciplined character belongs to the person who achieves balance by bringing all his faculties and powers under control. There are order, consistency, and purpose in his life. As a result he has poise and grace. He does not panic, nor does he indulge in maudlin self-pity when tossed by crosscurrents. He rises courageously, even heroically, to meet life and conquer it. He resolutely faces his duty. He is governed by a sense of responsibility. He has inward resources and personal reserves which are the wonder of weaker souls. He brings adversity under tribute, and compels it to serve him. When adversity becomes too overwhelming and blows fall which he cannot parry, he bows to them, but is not broken by them. His spirit still soars. The strong character of Madame Guyon enabled her, though imprisoned, to rise in spirit and sing:

> *My cage confines me round;*
> *Abroad I cannot fly.*
> *But though my wing is closely bound,*
> *My heart's at liberty.*
> *My prison walls cannot control*
> *The flight, the freedom of the soul.*

Of course there is power in such a life!
Furthermore, only the disciplined character can

carry through in the positions of larger responsibility. This is true in industry, education, religion. Many have ambitions which are never realized, goals which are never reached, aspirations for usefulness which are never fulfilled, visions which never materialize. While the failure may at times be due to limited ability, too often the deficiency is not in native endowment but in character. The capacity for grueling application is lacking. There may be the promising start, but not the discipline required to carry through. Even if by good fortune or "pull" the undisciplined man should reach the position of power, he cannot maintain it, for he is not inwardly prepared. He collapses under the weight of responsibility, and the pressure and complexity of detail. He lacks the strength of leadership, the fullness of knowledge, the soundness of judgment, which can only be built up bit by bit through years of painstaking toil.

Many a young person would like to become a doctor or a top-flight scientist but never will, simply because he will not buckle down to the demanding years of hard study. Many young people would like to achieve artistry and mastery in music but they never will, simply because they will not face the long hours of monotonous practice year after year. They may through natural talent become singers or pianists of a sort, but they will not pay that extra price for true excellence. They are too lazy and self-indulgent to pommel themselves to the top. Their ambitions may not be beyond their capacity, but they are beyond their discipline. The world is full of naturally brilliant people who never rise above mediocrity because they will not make the sacrifice which superiority requires.

I heard Igor Gorin, the famous Ukrainian-American baritone, admit in a radio interview that, while he started his conservatory training with a large class of promising young people, only one or two actually reached the top because, he said, the others were not willing to make the sacrifices that were required and submit themselves to the grind of years of rugged self-denial. Some fell in love and got married; some just became weary of the monotony and regimentation; others became homesick and returned home. Finally the ranks were thinned down to a very, very few. In the interview Mr. Gorin related a personal experience. He said that he had loved to smoke a pipe. But one day his professor of voice said to him, "Igor, you will have to make up your mind whether you are going to be a great singer or a great pipe smoker. You cannot be both." So the pipe went. Igor Gorin was willing to pay the price for mastery; others were not.

The edge possessed by the disciplined over the undisciplined shows up in many little things. The disciplined person picks up his clothes; the undisciplined lets them lie. One washes the bathtub after himself; the other leaves the high-water mark for someone else to scrub. One plans his work and works to his plan; the other works haphazardly. One is habitually prompt in his appointments; the other is notoriously tardy. Some people are always on time at church, while others never are. Observers of many years' experience will support the claim that the difference cannot be explained in the greater distance to travel or larger families to hustle. The difference is habit, and habit is character.

But the prizes go to the neat, the thoughtful, the systematic, the thrifty, the punctual. The brilliant lad who lives by his wits may dazzle his way to prominence, but sooner or later he is sure to sleep while the tortoise waddles past him. A boy who was far above average drifted nonchalantly through high school and early college. He wasn't going to let his education interfere with life! But toward the end of his college he settled down to serious studies; then he tried for a coveted scholarship which carried not only a large sum for advanced study but a coveted position in a reputable firm. Wanting just that position, in just that firm, he gave the effort all he had. In competition with many others he came first, with only one rival very close behind. The award went to the other lad—who came second. The manager explained kindly: "This position is one of great responsibility, and calls for steadiness and reliability. We find by studying your record that, though you have done well in this particular effort, your previous work has not been consistent. Better luck next time!" Those last words were a mere convention. The chagrined candidate stumbled out, knowing full well that luck had nothing to do with it. It was discipline that tipped the scale.

CHAPTER TWO

Discipline the Mark of Maturity

The term discipline carries a variety of meanings. To the child it means being compelled to do something undesirable and being punished if he rebels. Discipline for him means compulsion, pain, authority. To the soldier discipline means comformity to regulations, instant obedience to orders, K.P. duty, reveille on cold mornings. To the student it means the course of instruction he is undertaking, with the specific requirements and rules and examinations incident to it. I heard one man describe his academic qualifications in the words: "I submitted to the discipline of twelve units in psychology." To the Christian, discipline means *discipleship*—following Jesus, with one's self denied and one's cross resolutely carried.

The child, the soldier, the student, the disciple are all correct. But there is something more. The aim of child discipline, or military, or academic, or religious, is a *disciplined character* which goes beyond the minimum demands of these specific disciplines and permeates the whole life. Imposed discipline (of which we will say more later) must lead to self-discipline. It is even possible for the Christian to be a sincere and regenerated follower of Jesus, yet remain undisciplined in many facets of his character and in many areas of life. One may be a cross-bearer—one may, in fact, be purified from the carnal mind and filled with the Spirit—yet be merely on the threshold of that larger discipline of full maturity.

In a general sense, self-discipline is the ability to

regulate conduct by principle and judgment rather than impulse, desire, high pressure, or social custom. It is basically the ability to *subordinate.*

Appetites

There are several aspects here. For one thing, there is included the ability to subordinate the body and its physical appetites to the service of the mind. Paul said, "I keep my body under." This was exemplified by a fellow preacher who became convinced that coffee was affecting his heart. A Norwegian—mind you—who had enjoyed his coffee all his life! "But," he said, "that moment it became a matter of conscience with me. So I stopped." Just that simple. He hasn't touched it since. This ability was also seen in another friend who was fifty pounds overweight. When challenged by the doctor he resolutely embarked on a rugged diet which he maintained in all company, at all places and times, until his weight was normal—much to the improvement of his health. He explained simply, "It's not a question of will power, but of 'won't' power . . . No thank you, I won't have any." Such drastic adjustments are not always necessary, but the day-by-day discipline in many little things is. In truth we may say that the finest display of such discipline is not the spectacular achievement but the permanent adjustment of living pattern.

The subordination of the physical includes not only the appetite for food but also the sex urge. In some this has been so humored that it is abnormally excitable. To make matters worse, such persons often live by the creed of impotence: "I can't help it," and similar expressions of moral flabbiness. Overindulgence even within marriage may have the effect of cultivating this basic urge until it is increasingly imperious in its demands. Those so afflicted are in grave danger of succumbing to temptations from outside marriage when domestic stress, "frigidity" in their mates, long illness, or separations subject their enfeebled powers of self-control to an abnormal strain.

Too often the moral downfall of men is blamed on some failure in their wives. That is a cowardly evasion of moral responsibility. The man of disciplined character does not have to have a warm, responsive wife, who caters to his every impulse, to keep him in the path of virtue. He keeps himself there, by the grace of God. If his relationship with his wife is happy, he is grateful; if it is not, he simply appropriates more grace, and demonstrates the man that he is. A weak man is a poor risk no matter how warm is his wife; a strong man will keep himself pure even if it means total abstinence the rest of his life. And it must emphatically be affirmed that this is not just a matter of being "made that way" or natural temperament; it is a matter of achieving complete subordination.

Many marriages are less than ideal in their physical aspects. Some bodily or psychological impediment, some prolonged invalidism prevents the fulfillment of that romantic ideal in all its idyllic perfection. So what? Must there therefore be irritability and constant tension, and perpetual teetering on the brink of moral infidelity? Some apparently believe so. Such unideal conditions are often the rock on which the marriage is shattered. But they may also be the rock on which the marriage is built into a stronger and finer edifice. In these very problems a couple may find a deeper meaning of love and a truer, richer stability. They may feel the strain, of course, may even feel the undertow of temptation. But in that very situation they become conquerors of themselves in a new way and rise to new spiritual stature. They become gentler, nobler, spiritually taller. The marriage is not just "saved"; it is often stronger than marriages wherein there have been no deep struggles and decisive conquests.

It is true Paul warned the Corinthian married couples against subjecting one another to abnormal strain in this matter, lest they bring upon themselves over-powering temptations (I Corinthians 7). But the Corinthians, though truly converted, were still weak; they were far from the strength of mature, disciplined character. In fact they did not possess even the minimal foundation of entire sanctification.

Certainly Paul's advice is sound, and should be heeded by all married Christians out of tender mutual regard. But if peculiar circumstances make impossible the carrying out of this instruction, neither partner is thereby given grounds for making allowance for sin. It is good to heed the advice. It is still better to achieve that level of self-control which will make one morally triumphant even when the advice cannot be heeded. This is not an attempt to be "wise above what is written" but to maintain the moral standards which are the heart of what is written, when the practical application of the advice is shaped by the blunt facts of reality. Ralph G. Turnbull in A Minister's Obstacles relates the testimony of Dr. F. B. Meyer when a doctor came to him torn and tossed by sex temptation. In giving counsel "Meyer drew aside the curtain of his own life in self-revelation. His face was transfigured, and looking upward, he said with intense fervour, 'I have had a cross to bear in my life, and it has made me the man I am.' "

Emotions

Again, emotions must be subordinate to the reason. God wants all of us to be warmhearted. But the warm heart must have the wisdom of maturity, or it can become (or remain) the giddy impulsiveness of adolescence. When warmness is not disciplined, it tends to degenerate into irresponsible sentimentality, caprice, frivolity followed by depression—or even worse, flirting and philandering.

Too often the mind serves only the purpose of devising excuses for doing what the heart wants to do. The heart needs to be first cleansed, then kept on the leash of discipline. Then it can safely become the copartner with the mind in living according to fixed principles. The disciplined man has learned this art. He distrusts his sudden impulses. Not that he is cold and calculating; he may be warm and sympathetic; but he has grown up "into Christ" and is not "tossed to and fro, and carried about" either by "every wind of doctrine" or the winds of impulse, fancy, and strange feelings.

The emotions include the *affections*. Friendship, when based on mutual respect and understanding, is a beautiful gift. But true friendship is always a matter of increasingly deepening affection. When one suddenly awakens to a ripening affection which is either forbidden or dangerous, he has a real problem on his hands. Two friends may gradually become so "thick" that they become possessive and exclusive. Such inordinate affection is unwholesome and detrimental to both personality and character. Or an unmarried Christian may develop a friendship with an unregenerate person, at the office, or at school, or in some other perfectly natural and legitimate relationship. At first there is no thought of love. In fact the Christian may even be motivated by an honest desire to help the other spiritually. But if the two are thrown more and more together, gradually that may steal into their hearts which lights the eye and quickens the pulse at the other's presence. Then the Christian will have to face a terrible emotional struggle to become extricated or an unscriptural marriage will result.

An even more dangerous peril can exist in the friendship between married Christians of the opposite sex. Their work (even the Lord's work) may legitimately throw them into each other's company. We can think of many such teams: doctor-nurse, singer-pianist, executive-secretary, pastor-deaconess, floorwalker-saleslady, superintendent-teacher, and many others. Modern society being what it is, we as Christians are not apt to be able always to avoid situations in which we are thrown into close activity with persons of the opposite sex. Duty often demands such co-working.

Working with persons of the opposite sex may bring mutual distrust and dislike; there is no great peril in that. But working together may bring respect, mutual confidence, and comradeship. So far, so good. Such friendships may be holy and beautiful on a brother-sister basis. But a certain reserve and distance must be preserved at all costs, and will be by men and women of disciplined character. Friendship can become affection, affection love, love lust, and the progress be a shock to both. That which was begun innocently may end disastrously.

The rugged advice of Jesus to pluck out the offending eye, or cut off the hand or foot, is never more apropos than in this kind of situation. Souls, homes, happiness, influence—all will be saved only by drastic, even ruthless, action. The feelings must not be spared. No quarter must be given. Here again Christians must tolerate not the least vestige of the philosophy of impotence: "I can't help it." Emotions may not immediately obey the will, but actions must. In due course, by the grace of God, emotions will follow the lead of disciplined adjustment, strong purpose, and decisive stand.

A friend was once very deeply in love with a young woman, to whom he proposed marriage. But she married another. The rejected suitor found that his affection was still fixed on her, though she was now another man's wife. At first it seemed he must go through life tortured with a love which could never be returned. His feeling seemed entirely beyond his control. But knowing this was wrong, he took himself in hand. He said, "It is wrong for me to love her—I don't have to love her—and by God's grace I *won't!*" It was not easy. But he deliberately fought the battle through, on his knees and in his heart, until gradually his strong affection subsided, and he was able to put her out of his heart and mind completely and forever. He later was happily married to another, and is today a successful, noble minister. It was the victory of heroic manliness.

Such is an example of the triumph of disciplined character. Without such ruggedness there will be maudlin self-pity and moral deterioration. With it one can face the moral hazards of life and rise to higher and higher heights of strength and nobility. But the finest discipline of all is not that which struggles out of a near-tragic situation, but foresees and forestalls the situation in the first place. The young Christian who adopts certain basic principles respecting friendships, and avoids making intimate alliances with the unsaved, will not have the battle with tumultuous desires and affections later on. And the married Christian worker who is ever alert to the perils which beset him, and is self-disciplined always in look and word and action, will not ignite fires which he will have to fight feverishly to put out.

Moods

Disciplined character also means the mastery of moods. This is yet another area of conquest in the subordination of one's emotions. Actually, the need here is twofold. First, we must cultivate that fixedness of purpose, that steadiness of faith, that quiet, almost rhythmic, performance of duty, which gradually chastens our moods, cleansing from them their fierce wildness and bringing them into keeping with our total pattern. Then our moods will fluctuate less often and certainly less radically. The pendulum, even if it still swings, will not swing so far.

Secondly, we must learn to transcend the moods which we cannot entirely elude. Some ebb and flow of feeling is inevitable. Some slight shifting of interest or attitude is apt to occur in the steadiest personality. A failure in our work combined with physical weariness may bring a cloud of depression and discouragement. A windy day, a letter from home, a personal misunderstanding are some of the many little things which play on our spirits and produce some variations in our feelings —possibly a touch of nostalgia or loneliness. With the changed mood may come strange impulses which we dare not heed—maybe to take a trip, or make an unwise purchase, or neglect some duty—impulses which will not pass one's common sense in sober moments. With the changed mood also may come the temptation to let our mood show. There is danger of appearing suddenly altered in our relationships with the people around us. According to the mood we may be abnormally gay and open or morose and close, generous to the point of profligacy or prudent to the point of stinginess. One day we may be optimistic, the next day pessimistic. Because our personalities cannot be relied upon for consistency, our friends do not know what to expect next. At first people are puzzled. Then they learn to say, "Just one of his moods"—with a hint of scorn. And they learn to be wary and apprehensive in all relationships with us, for they never quite know what mood they will find us in, or how soon our mood will change.

Such a tendency to exhibit moodiness is a grave weakness. The mature person learns to apply himself to the regular tasks of life with a consistent "face" in spite of varying moods. The wife or husband, the teacher, the executive, the secretary, the pastor, the janitor, the singer, who can be counted on to be temperamentally even and reliable, always the same in cheerful, cooperative attitudes, regardless of feelings, circumstances, or weather, will have a steadily accelerating influence over others. All will sense that here is a person of quiet strength, even though they may not be able to analyze the secret.

It is said that a Christian once asked Amanda Smith what she should do when a cloud settled down over her spirit. The colored saint replied, "What do you do when you are setting the table and a shadow falls across the room?"

The lady answered, "I just take a quick look to see if a serious storm is brewing, and if not I go right on setting the table."

"Do exactly the same," admonished Mrs. Smith. "When a cloud comes over your soul, take a quick look to see if sin has brought darkness. If you find no sin, just go right on setting the table for the Lord!" That is mastering our moods. That, too, is growing up.

A mature, disciplined Christian has learned "to feel just as good when he feels bad as he does when he feels good"—in the Lord; and in the quiet, steady application of his energies to life.

Disciplined character never dissipates time and energy by catering to moodiness. "I don't feel like it" may at times express the plain truth, but the habitual use of this phrase is the trait of the weakling, not the strong man. When a college student explained that he had not attended the last class session because he "didn't feel like it," the professor said: "Young man, has it ever occurred to you that most of the world's work is done by people who 'don't feel like it'?"

Speech

Regardless of how carefully controlled a person is at all other points, none can qualify for the high rating of a truly disciplined character whose tongue is not restrained by the bridle of prudence and directed by the reins of love. And this is scriptural. "If any man among you seem to be religious, and bridleth not his tongue, but deceiveth his own heart, this man's religion is vain" (Jas. 1:26). One may have a disciplined body, a disciplined mind, a disciplined will, even disciplined emotions, appetites, and habits, but a loose tongue betrays a fatal fault in the armor. The character is defective.

Some people pride themselves on their frankness. "I say what I think," they boast. So does the fool, according to the Bible: "A fool uttereth all his mind." Frankness is indeed a virtue when coupled with intelligent, loving tact and discretion. But it becomes a sadistic vice when it is merely the unbridled eruptings of opinions without regard to times and places or human feelings. "There is that speaketh like the piercings of a sword: but the tongue of the wise is health" (Prov. 12:18). It often takes a far higher display of discipline to refrain from speaking than it does to speak. Forbearance is a Christian virtue, even as is frankness.

The Bible has an astonishing amount to say about the control of the tongue. James clearly makes it the archstone of disciplined living: "If any man offend not in word, the same is a perfect man, and able also to bridle the whole body" (Jas. 3:2). Admittedly, this is a level of perfection which few have reached, but it is within reach of all; and such discretion in the speech should be included in our vision of the disciplined character.

Priorities

Furthermore, a truly disciplined character has the ability to subordinate the lesser to the greater. Here is the problem of priorities—probably the most crucial problem of life. On its solution hang success or failure, improvement or degeneration, and in the larger sense, heaven or hell.

The battle here is not primarily to achieve a clear perception of what is more important, for all Christians acknowledge that God and His Church should hold first place in our lives. Without hesitation we would concede that heaven is an infinitely richer goal than earthly position, that persons come before profits, that the culture of the soul and the mind is more to be desired than entertainment, that character is of far greater value than pleasure, that usefulness is better than idleness, that

soul winning is life's crowning achievement, that righteousness is infinitely more satisfying than popularity.
When confronted bluntly with these simple alternatives
we know instantly which to approve. We would say,
"Yes, these are the supreme values, and to realize them
is my supreme goal." The problem therefore is not
knowledge. The problem is actually giving first place
to these values in practical daily living—and that is a
problem primarily of character.

This involves ability to reject day by day that great
army of possible activities which clamor for our precious
energy but which would hamper the doing of more important things. All of us are confronted by a bewildering
multiplicity of claims upon our time, talent, money, and
loyalties. The claims are not only legion, but loud and
insistent. To attempt to satisfy even half of them would
result in frittering life away to nothingness. If life with
us is to be fruitful and purposeful, we must heroically
and decisively put the knife to most of the possible activities which could clutter every single day.

Selection—selection—selection! This is the law of
life. We cannot join everything; therefore we must select. We cannot participate in every good cause; therefore we must select. We cannot give to everything;
therefore we must select. We cannot go to every interesting concert or lecture or meeting; therefore we must
select. We cannot read everything; therefore we must
select.

To become well read is vastly more than reading;
it is a matter of exclusion as well as inclusion. President
Case of Boston University once said: "If you want to
become a specialist in New Testament literature, you
must say good-by to the comics forever." And to a lot
of other reading too! Whatever one's goal may be, it can
be achieved only by the sacrifice of the lesser. This
requires discipline of a high order.

Our stature as men and women, certainly our stature

as Christians, will be determined exactly and entirely by our skill in selecting. If we give top priority to those pursuits which should have low priority, if we "major in minors," if we show a "first-rate dedication to second-rate causes," if we allow friends and impulse and the convenience of the moment to dictate our priorities, while we weakly drift with the tide of daily circumstance, we will be shabby, mediocre, and ineffective persons.

If we affirm certain priorities but fail to give them first place day by day; if we allow them to remain in the "never-never-land" of good intentions, without rigid adherence *right now*—the end result of character-zero will be just as sure. *Now* we must say "yes" to this and "no" to that. *Now* we must put first things first. And we must do it no matter how much more pleasant and appealing other things may be at the moment. It is reported that when a professional author said to Sir Winston Churchill that he couldn't write unless the "mood" came on him, the great statesman replied: "No! shut yourself in your study from nine to one and make yourself write. Prod yourself!—kick yourself!—it's the only way."

This level of discipline will enable the reader of a fiction thriller to lay it down when duty calls; he will not be so captivated that all else is neglected. It will enable its possessor to labor in the summer, not fritter away the golden hours and then panic when winter threatens. It will push its possessor out of bed when he yet has time to get to work without rush, which is much better than dawdling another half hour and then regretting it the rest of the day. Or *she* will make the bed and do the dishes in the morning, rather than allow afternoon hours to find her wishing she had, and maybe in tears because of the neglected housework that suddenly stares her in the face. And the student will settle down to study early in the semester, rather than drift and play until looming exams send him into feverish, midnight cramming. "Prod yourself!—kick yourself!—it's the only way."

Adjustment to Authority

The final hallmark of the disciplined character is the ability to assimilate imposed discipline with grace and profit. It is by no means easy to subordinate natural initiative and self-assertion to legitimate authority. But it must be done if one expects maximum happiness and usefulness, and if one desires to achieve a mature character. Rebellion at times may be one's clear duty. But in most of life's normal relationships rebellion is stupid and destructive. Being a constitutional rebel is no ground for pride. Habitual rebellion is the cult of weaklings rather than the strong. It requires neither intelligence nor character to assert loudly, "No one can tell me what to do." But it requires both to submit to the inescapable and necessary constraints of society; and submit, not grudgingly, but graciously, with mature understanding and cheerful good will.

The unbroken colt is of little value. Whatever value he has is based on the assumption that he will not remain unbroken. The person who finds his true place and worth is the person who learns to wear the yoke. When a young man or woman intelligently learns that life is a bundle of relationships involving give as well as take, subordination as well as domination, that moment is his or her value to society compounded many fold. This is exemplified first in the home, then in school, then in the church, then in one's vocation. Whether one is a lawyer, or doctor, or railroad engineer, or office clerk—no matter where or how one works, there are rules, or codes of ethics, or government regulations, or superior levels of authority in the form of employers, boards, managers, superintendents, *et cetera,* to which one must submit. If we are constantly kicking and chafing, we will be unhappy, to say the least, and in danger of becoming drifters. Insubordination, selfishness, misery, and uselessness are bedfellows.

The Christian, of course, must make sure he does not

confuse such subordination to imposed discipline with blind, unthinking submission to the wishes and opinions of everyone about him. Proper submission to legitimate authority by no means extends to conformity to the world. Even that spirit of submission which Christian wives are to manifest toward unsaved husbands, and which is such an acid test of the wife's spiritual maturity, is not to be interpreted as requiring obedience to demands which violate her conscience as a Christian.

Then, in the larger circles, such as in the world of fashion and custom, a fine independence of spirit, opinion, and practice is a noble thing. Discipline does not require that we be echoes only. The wise Christian must learn to submit to some yokes, but throw off others. If there must be dictation at all in matters of personal life and fashion, it had better come from the church than from the world. But even the church must not dictate too much. Christians must find their way between extreme nonconformity and extreme subjugation. They must learn to draw the line before proper assimiliation of imposed discipline becomes extinction of private thinking and personal initiative. Insubordination is bad, but individuality is good.

It takes careful thinking to discriminate between distortion and normalcy in all of these facets of Christian discipline. But the essential fact is clear: Discipline is the mark of maturity. Without discipline the character will remain weak and infantile.

CHAPTER THREE

The Perils of Discipline

To build up the virtues of disciplined living until it almost seems to be the *summum bonum* of life, then talk about its perils, may appear contradictory. It is like the antibiotic which is hailed as a virtual miracle drug but which proves to have deadly side effects.

Fortunately the deadly side effects of discipline are only possible; they are not inevitable. They can be avoided. But to avoid them we must know them. What could possibly be perilous in this which seems to be such an unmixed blessing?

A Christian Perspective

The peril of seriously thinking that discipline is the supreme value of life is possibly the greatest of all. It is not the supreme value. Right relationship with God is the greatest of all treasures. Divine grace, forgiveness, the divine presence, love, faith—these are more elemental, more indispensable. Discipline must never be elevated to the place of honor; that must be reserved for Christ. Discipline must be seen as a servant, not a savior. It is nothing more or less than a practical means of learning how to realize more fully in one's life the supreme values of Christ's kingdom.

If we avoid this first peril, we are more apt to avoid the second: the peril of pride. Discipline unquestionably makes a man superior. If not watched, it will also make him *feel* superior. There is a legitimate sense of satisfaction in self-mastery. But it is wrong when the sense of satisfaction becomes *self*-satisfaction. Such a disciplined man gives himself the glory, not God. He admires the character which he himself has fashioned. With this smugness will likely be snobbery. When a man is proud of his discipline, he disdains the common rabble. When the virtue of discipline is thus allowed to feed the vice of pride, the virtue itself becomes a snare. It is a delusion as complete as the self-deception of the Pharisee who congratulated himself in the guise of prayer: "Father, I thank thee that I am not as other men are . . ." A most repugnant character is the self-made man who is loquaciously proud of his handiwork.

The Danger of Extremes

There is also the peril of extremes. Two extremes tempt the valiant soul who desires to incorporate ruggedness into life. One is in the realm of imposed discipline; we may call it unchristian severity. The other is in the realm of self-discipline: unchristian asceticism.

All who exercise authority over others, particularly in the training of young people and children, are in danger of severity to the point of cruelty. It is possible to clap children and youth under a prisonlike rule which hardens without strengthening. Or it forces them into molds for which they are not fitted. John Wesley's experiment in training children at Kingswood Hill failed dismally because his principles of discipline were too rigid. Forbidding all play (ages six to twelve), requiring a 4:00 a.m. rising, fasting until after 3:00 p.m. on Fridays, and the study (no electives) of reading, writing, arithmetic, English, French, Latin, Greek, Hebrew, history, geography, chronology, rhetoric, logic, ethics, geometry, algebra, physics, and music, would produce either monks or maniacs!

Unchristian Asceticism

But if those who are inclined to be strict with others need to avoid unwise severity, so those who are inclined to be Spartan with themselves need to avoid unchristian asceticism. There is a reasonable abstemiousness and temperance which must be cultivated. But there is a point beyond which self-inflicted rigor becomes unwholesome—when it becomes counterfeit discipline. Unchristian discipline is much more showy and exacting than plodding Christian discipline. It is more radical and thorough, and therefore poses as superior. But in the end it is a blind alley. It promises much but produces little. It does not lead to that warm, vibrant nobility of character which is our Christian goal.

How can Christian discipline be distinguished from pagan asceticism? At several points: Asceticism calls attention to itself; discipline does not. Asceticism fastens its prohibitions and rules on objects which in themselves are petty; discipline deals largely with those things which are ethically potent and relevant. Asceticism tends to despise the good things of life. It denies joys and experiences which are the gifts of God, and which God intended should be received. This is due to the germ of dualism which lies in the heart of unchristian asceticism: that matter is evil, that life is a misfortune, that the body is a shame, and that holiness consists of complete denial of everything earthly and physical.

In contrast Christian discipline never despises earthly blessings, but consecrates them to spiritual ends. It permits their use with thanksgiving, but not their abuse. It sanctifies the physical by restraint and direction, offering the whole to God for sacrifice or service. It will not bow in slavery to the senses, but neither will it destroy them as evil. Its hallmark is not abstinence from God's gifts, but temperance; but more than temperance, complete dedication to God's glory.

True Christian discipline may at times deny itself God's good gifts as rigorously as a hermit, but such denial will not be a means to holiness but a means of service. It will be practiced, not because the thing sacrificed is believed to be evil, but because the sacrifice in this particular instance is helpful in achieving a yet greater good. Some evangelists deliberately sacrifice marriage in order to be free to evangelize more effectively. In doing so they are casting no reflection on marriage itself; they are not rejecting marriage per se. Their celibate life is neither a mark of holiness nor a means to holiness; it is simply a practical means to a greater liberty in roving evangelism.

What About St. Paul?

Paul too was a celibate. Often the great Apostle to the Gentiles is singled out as an example of asceticism. We are reminded that he "kept his body under" and that he spoke of "fastings oft"; and some insist that he even recommended celibacy as the preferable and proper way of life. This we deny. Other things being equal, postponement of marriage, he told the Corinthians, would be advisable "for the present distress." Elsewhere he repudiated those who forbade marriage, just as he also repudiated extremists who demanded abstinence from meat. On the grounds of Christian charity, yes: "If meat make my brother to offend, I will eat no flesh while the world standeth" (I Cor. 8:13). But not on the grounds that meat eating is in itself an evil because it caters to the appetites of the body; for he pronounced the verdict: "Every creature of God is good, and . . . [is to] be received with thanksgiving" (I Tim. 3:4).

True, he said, "Make not provision for the flesh, to fulfil the lusts thereof" (Rom. 13:14). But even a cursory study of the context will show that he meant, "Make no provision to satisfy the illicit desires of an unsanctified carnal nature." To construe him as forbidding the legitimate satisfaction of natural appetites within the framework of God's law would be involving the apostle in a denial of life itself. Taken thus literally, the command would imply the cessation of all labor, and men would

starve; for what is honest toil but the act of making provision for the hunger of the body? No, while Paul was
an admirable example of Christian discipline, he cannot
be cited as either an example or an advocate of extreme
asceticism. No man saw more clearly the vanity of mere
asceticism as a means to holiness—a point which will be
mentioned again later.

Undisciplined Discipline

Another peril must be given very thoughtful attention: the deadly danger of undisciplined discipline. It
admittedly takes high discipline to develop certain basic
habits which safeguard the soul. But once the habits are
established it takes just as much discipline to see that
they do not become tyrants. Habit must be kept to the
role of servant; otherwise it becomes the master, and the
personality begins to vegetate.

A growing soul is ever changing. The kind of discipline desired is not that which embeds the life in a
concrete block of fixed routine, so that the new shoots of
fresh ideas and new undertakings and exciting discov-
eries cannot get through; but the kind which exists only
to shed the old forms of death, and exclude the unpro-
ductive suckers, in order that life's new challenges can be
seized and exploited to the full. The discipline of the
Pharisees was too rigid; it was indeed the old wineskin
which was incapable of holding the new wine of the
Kingdom. So the Pharisees were betrayed by their very
virtue—their discipline. That which should have best
fitted them for the kingdom of God kept them out. A
higher form of discipline is that which grows and adjusts
and expands with life itself; it is only the lower discipline which congeals into a static perfection. Therefore it is well to give some thought to the discipline of
discipline. It too must be subordinate.

Who does not admire the man who with superb
powers of "mind over mattress" arises at five every

morning to pray? With rugged self-whippings he establishes the practice as a life pattern, to which all else must bend. If it is possible he should resolutely hold to his rule. But suppose traveling, or a few unavoidably late nights, or domestic illness, means that to continue to rise at five will result in faltering efficiency, raw nerves, foggy judgment, sleepy-eyed yawns when duty demands alertness, then a sick spell, with a resultant loss of work and dislocated finances, and added burdens on the poor wife, already overworked, who must now run a hospital because her husband, with a stubborn but unwise courage, determined to stick to his rule. A more intelligent discipline would be to adjust until the special circumstances passed, then resume the routine as soon as practicable; or, if necessary, abandon it altogether in favor of some other provision for prayer and blessing. God's dispensations of grace are not confined to five o'clock in the morning.

An evangelist observed fasting on Wednesday and Friday for many years without variation under any circumstances. After several months of absence he came home to an eager, Daddy-hungry family. When they excitedly sat down to eat, the first meal as an unbroken family circle in all that time, he returned thanks, then left the table and shut himself in his room; it was his fast day. The gloom of disappointment settled down on the uncomprehending children. From one standpoint that would appear to be heroic self-denial. I am wondering if it was not rather a slavish bondage to habit. Even if self-denial was present, it is certain that in a still larger measure family-denial was present also. A higher discipline would have scorned the tyranny of petty rule, and would have dictated eating with his wife and children a happy, hearty meal, then resuming the routine of fasting when he left for the next revival.

In disciplining our discipline we must not only keep our habit patterns subordinate to life but we must learn to absorb the interruptions of life, and where possible turn them to good account. We might call this an intelligent flexibility and resiliency. No matter how well we may order ourselves in creating fixed patterns and routines, we cannot control the unexpected events which demand constant adjustment. Some people cannot adjust quickly. They either refuse to face reality, and hence charge right on through, often hurting others; or else, having adjusted to the unexpected demand, they are completely disorganized and demoralized for the rest of the day. They cannot get back on the track. In these two types we have the unbending, poker backbone and the collapsing, string backbone—which is no backbone at all. But in neither extreme do we see a display of true discipline.

It is a mistake to suppose that disciplined living is entirely a matter of rigid rule, routine, and habit; or that its highest exhibition is in being able to determine a course of action for the day and then batter one's way through at any cost. Too many other people and legitimate demands are apt to get trampled upon by that kind of obstinacy. Such self-discipline is too akin to bullheadedness and self-will. It may be a symptom of basic selfishness.

This may shock some, since they have struggled so hard to bring some semblance of order into their lives and cultivate a healthy respect for the clock. They know that only in rigid regimentation of time and energy will they reach maximum accomplishment. Having achieved a measure of such control, they want above all to keep the reins in a tight grip, and they expect the world to stand aside and allow them to drive their well-ordered chariot through undisturbed. When the world jostles in and slows the horses and rocks the chariot, they are apt to be petulant. To whip the horses right on, brushing aside the intrusions and riding over the obstacles, is in their view a mark of strength. But there is a higher kind of strength. It is the ability to adjust without being deflected, to pause without stopping all day.

Far more important than our hidebound little systems are *people*. Helping people should be the supreme objective of all our self-discipline. The trains that are built to carry people should not run them down. The story is told of a young man who faced a judge who reprimanded him in these words: "Ought not you to be ashamed of yourself for being before me on such a serious charge—you whose father is a famous and highly respected jurist?" Bitterly the young man replied: "No, I am not ashamed. When I was younger and wanted his companionship and would sometimes seek to get his attention, he would always say: 'Go away, boy, I am too busy writing my book, *The Law of Trusts*.' Now he has his book, *The Law of Trusts*, and here am I." That father forgot that parenthood itself was a trust. It took self-discipline to hold himself to the task of writing his book, but in so doing he neglected a greater duty.

The value of orderliness is by no means depreciated. That kind of discipline which whips the life into shape is absolutely essential. Often it is heroic, and always it is admirable; but only as a means to ends beyond itself, not as an end in itself. A disciplined character just for the sake of a disciplined character can be as vain and useless as an undisciplined character. The end must be a larger usefulness, and to this one aim all the various strands of discipline must be compelled to pay tribute. The self-denial in achieving this discipline, the restraint of impulse, the lashing of indolence are commendable; but ignoring people and their immediate needs in order to protect our idealistic program is not commendable. For our relationships as human beings must always take precedence over our relationships as automatons.

CHAPTER FOUR

Discipline and Holiness

Further perils respecting discipline are found in the attempt to relate it to holiness. Here the human heart is prone to make four mistakes.

Discipline Is Not Holiness

One mistake is to *confuse disciplined living with holy living.* The two are not the same. Holiness is a religious reality which transcends self in its terms of reference. Discipline, on the other hand, may begin and end with self-interest. Holiness is meaningless except as it defines one's relationship to a holy God, and one's moral state in the sight of that God. It is possible for a man to achieve disciplined living while bypassing God altogether. God may not be in his thoughts at all. But in holiness God is never out of them.

Athletes, who may follow a rugged program of self-regimentation and denial which puts the average Christian to shame, are an example. They do it, Paul says, for an earthly crown, but we "an heavenly." When discipline is linked with heaven as its aim, it becomes linked with holiness, but not until then.

The businessman, also, may deny both body and soul in his total consecration to mammon. In the process he may live purely and simply, but only because such a life better serves his aim. The rich man of our Lord's parable said to himself, "Take thine ease," implying in all probability that he had never taken his ease before. Very likely he had hated indolence and self-indulgence. He had worshiped at the shrine of hard work, of frugality and industry, of early rising and long days. He had spurned idling his hours "in his cups." He had been a model of good citizenship—hard-working, sober, prosperous. But God called him a fool. He had discipline without holiness. From him to whom much is given shall much be required. He to whom the capacity is given to achieve disciplined living will be required to answer at the judgment for the lack of holy living.

Statesmen, politicians, teachers, scholars, physicians, artists, and musicians can readily be found who have reached the top through dint of diligent discipline over long years, but who are far from God. It is even possible to be a pleasure seeker, the very epitome of uselessness and selfishness, yet in the quest for pleasure live a self-controlled and regular life. The thoroughgoing epicurean who frankly is after all the pleasure in life he can get may live as simply and spotlessly as a hermit. For if he is to gain maximum pleasure he must avoid pain. As William Henry Roberts puts it: "This rules out at once any mere yielding to every impulse. The wise man will look ahead and look around . . . When we scrutinize life so carefully, dissipation, violence, and extravagance of every kind lose all allure."[1] Why? Because dissipation, violence, and extravagance are wrong? No, but because they bring more pain than pleasure. Therefore the epicurean eschews any form of intemperance. His motives are no better than those which prompt the drunken libertine; his sagacity is sharper, that's all.

Sometimes observing young people are puzzled by such amiable, even-tempered, kindly neighbors (who are equally as careful to avoid being filled with the Spirit as they are being drunk with wine), and are tempted to compare them unfavorably with Christians whose lives are more volcanic, not nearly as pretty and contained. But we must never prefer the gardener in his garden to the soldier in the battle if the enemy is at the gates and

[1]*The Problem of Choice*, p. 142.

every man is needed. The gentle gardener is seen then, not as superior, but as simply selfish and irresponsible. So likewise is the well-regulated, disciplined life of the neighborly epicurean a sham. The striving Christian may not yet have achieved an equal discipline, but he at least has broken out of his tight little circle of self and linked up with the world's greatest cause.

Discipline Not a Substitute

Closely allied with this first mistake is the *second:* the tragic error of allowing discipline to be a *substitute for holiness.* The man who has himself under perfect control is very apt to be satisfied. He has proved himself the master—what other master does he need? There are souls who are sharp enough to see the utilitarian value of a well-regulated, conventionally impeccable life, who are not big enough to be aware that life has a third dimension. They are too small. They are content with a narrow little respectability, lending an aura of dignity to their creature comforts. Wrapped in their garments of self-righteousness they seem impervious to any sense of lack. They don't need to repent, for they have no vices. They avoid every extravagance. They are correct in their deportment, honest in their business, habits are well ordered, life is tidy and well arranged. They know when to stop eating, they get to bed sensibly and get up early. They are primly and precisely proper.

But they are not deep enough to be torn by profound questions of death and immortality, of sin, truth, duty, God. They are not haunted by a sense of guilt. They are not beset by a hunger and thirst after righteousness. Their only obsession is to avoid all such distressing notions. They wish for nothing more than to be let alone, and dread nothing more than such painful intrusions into the even tenor of their ways.

It is hard indeed to penetrate the defenses of these smugly content, self-assured people. One can verily believe they have been aided in their discipline by the devil himself. At least their discipline has become their damnation. The discipline which snubs God and thereby shrivels the soul into a neat little ball of respectability becomes a monstrous thing. It is like the juggler who captivates your attention as he picks your pocket. It opens the door of earth while it bars the gates of heaven.

Discipline Not the Way to Holiness

But if accepting discipline as a substitute for holiness is the mistake of the irreligious, the *third* error is the mistake of the religious. I refer to the age-old assumption that discipline is the *means to holiness.* This assumption underlies monasticism and asceticism. In fact discipline as a means to holiness becomes asceticism. Much devotional literature is honeycombed with this infatuation. It is a delusion which dies hard. Without doubt disciplined living is a necessary aid in maintaining holiness and consolidating it into firm character and efficient living. But no amount of discipline of itself *will make the sinful heart holy.* It may shackle specific sins; it may apparently imprison the disease and limit its activity. But it cannot create a clean heart.

Paul was clear here in writing to the Colossians. He remonstrates: "Why do you submit to regulations, do not handle, do not taste, do not touch (referring to things which all perish as they are used), according to human precepts and doctrines?" Then he puts his finger on the fallacy: "These have indeed an appearance of wisdom in promoting rigor of devotion and self-abasement and severity to the body, but they are of no value in checking the indulgence of the flesh" (Col. 2: 23, R.S.V.). Those who seek holiness via asceticism take a sort of grim glee in their austerity, and progressively multiply rules and prohibitions about pettier and pettier trifles until they are as bound as Lazarus in his graveclothes. Their pride is fed, their spirit is crystallized into a harsh legalism, and life becomes a tomb; but in the meanwhile they do not achieve holiness.

The basic reason for the impotence of discipline in attaining holiness is inbred sin. The psychology of sin described in Romans 7 may be far from modern jargon, but it is true to human experience. There the sin principle is seen as a deep-seated perversity which is ineradicable by either self-culture or the enforcement of law. It is an irrational twist which baffles the moralist by eluding every attempt at dislodgment. In fact Paul uses language which comes near implying that sin is a thing—almost as if it might be isolated under the microscope. His language means no more than that sinfulness is deeper than an act—that it is a persistent tendency in man's total nature; but that it is an alien quality, which no more belongs there than tangles in a child's hair; and that it is beyond the power of man to remove. To repeat: its cure is beyond either externally imposed law or self-imposed discipline.

A stray black spaniel once pretended to "adopt" us. He was a fine, healthy, friendly specimen. After trying without success to find an owner, we designated ourselves as such by buying a dog license, a fine collar, and a leash. Legally he was ours. He was openly identified as ours—the license on the collar proclaimed the fact. But we soon learned that only the continued restraint of the leash would prevent his compulsive wanderings. After several days of such restraint, during which time we would feed him well and pet him and play with him, we would be confident that he was now cured of his wanderlust and would stay home. But the moment he was free from "law," off he would bound down the street to play with another dog, completely deaf to our commanding and coaxing. Only hunger would bring him home. Finally even that failed, and he went for good, license and all. The law had chained him but had not changed him. In fact the law had more quickly and decisively revealed what he really was at heart—a tramp dog.

The inspired apostle insists, and experience verifies, that as futile as were our attempts in the canine world, so are all attempts in the world of human character to discipline the rebellious heart into inward holiness. The carnal heart is like a balloon: squeeze it with the finger of discipline in one place and it will only stretch a little bigger somewhere else.

Suffering Does Not Sanctify

As slow as we are to abandon hope in the discipline of law (either God-imposed, society-imposed, or self-imposed), we are even slower to give up trusting in the discipline of *suffering*. Poets seem to assume that all that is needed to make us pious is more pain. Tears have power to wash the very soul, it is believed. But the poets forget that the suffering that seems both to soften and strengthen some hardens and weakens others. The suffering of Fantine in *Les Miserables* did not make a refined, gentle saint but a desperate, haggard harlot, who could snarl and scratch like a cat.

It is true that Hebrews reads: "For they verily for a few days chastened us after their own pleasure; but he for our profit, that we might be partakers of his holiness. Now no chastening for the present seemeth to be joyous, but grievous: nevertheless afterward it yieldeth the peaceable fruit of righteousness unto them which are exercised thereby" (Heb. 12:10-11). Here we have chastening and holiness linked in what appears to be a cause-and-effect relationship. Righteousness is the "peaceable fruit" (a sort of chain reaction) of suffering. Such indeed is God's hope and purpose in allowing it. But there is a link in the chain which, while not stated, is assumed. Suffering is intended, not to be the purifying agent, but to drive the soul to Him who is. Suffering prior to holiness serves one great purpose: it shows us our helplessness, our littleness, our insecurity, our need of God. Like the law, it shows us our self-will and rebellion. It shows us the folly of the proud head and the stiff neck. It thus makes us wiser—wise enough (such is the hope) to yield utterly to God in contrite brokenness, and let His grace transform us within.

No, holiness is inwrought by the Holy Spirit, not because we have suffered, but because we have surrendered. It is inwrought in response to our faith—faith, not in our tears, but in His blood. It is inwrought, not by our struggling, but by His power, when we cease writhing and begin resting. The blood of the atonement, the power of the Spirit, the Word of God, *plus* the catalyst of faith—these are the secrets of soul cleansing. And discipline, whether it be the discipline of law, training, or suffering, must never be allowed to usurp the place of any single one of these. Faith can release in a moment powers for holiness that discipline cannot command in a millennium.

Discipline, then, is not the path to purity and it can never substitute for the grace of God in entire sanctification, received by faith.

Holiness Is the Foundation

But exactly what *is* the place of discipline in the life of holiness? What is the relationship? In answer it can be said that entire sanctification is the secret of successful Christian discipline, and in return, maintained discipline is a necessary aid in maintaining holiness. Clearly there is an interaction between the two. Now that the false relationships have been torn away, we can more accurately determine what the true relationship is. We have mistakenly labored under the delusion that holiness is the fruition of discipline. It is not; it is the foundation.

1. For one thing, the *imposed* disciplines of life will not be as readily assimilated and transmuted into char-

acter as they ought to be until the irrational resistance to discipline is removed from the heart. A certain measure of combativeness may be essential to healthy personality; but when the combativeness is aggravated by inbred sin, it becomes an irritable "set" against all restraint. A student, or child, or church member, or citizen, so afflicted may outwardly submit while inwardly seething, like the little girl who was forcibly compelled by her father to sit down in her chair but defiantly said, "I may be sitting down on the outside but I am standing up on the inside." The inward tension and resentment neutralize any character benefit which might normally accrue from the discipline.

This psychological block is *irrational* because the resistance is not intelligent opposition to specific disciplines which in themselves are wrong, but impulsive and habitual opposition to all restraint, right or wrong, and particularly that restraint or opposition which may happen to cross one's desires and impulses of the moment. A serious injustice, or a repression which becomes an unlawful oppression, might well be resisted. But when there is deep in the heart something that rebels at parents or teachers or circumstances—even God—when personal will is thwarted, then the state of the heart is not normal, but diseased.

A young woman, a Christian, resented her pastor's necessary counseling at a point of church discipline and exclaimed: "I cannot stand interference in my life." Now as long as there is such a block in the nature— conscious or subconscious—mature, disciplined character will be impossible. But the breaking down of that sort of stoniness, the removal of such an inward impediment, is exactly what a genuine experience of entire sanctification will accomplish. The soul in a new humility and teachableness will now be adjusted to the *idea* of imposed discipline, and with this changed attitude will begin assimilating *specific* disciplines with a new spirit of gratitude. One will even seek to profit by the bits of unfairness that get mixed up with the discipline now and again.

2. Entire sanctification will not only orient the soul to imposed discipline but impart the impulse to *self-discipline,* in case that impulse has been lacking previously. There will be a desire for orderliness, efficiency, improvement. A half-caste aboriginal woman in Australia had been inclined to drift with the indolent habits of her people, but after entering into a deep experience of God's grace she said: "Now I always undress when I go to bed." In that statement, related as it was to God's purifying grace, you have the secret of civilizing backward peoples anywhere in the world. It must be from the inside out, and must begin with a desire no longer to take the easy way of least resistance but to live a disciplined life.

3. Furthermore, the sanctifying grace of God will provide the dynamic for *sustained* discipline. The impulse is not enough. There must be power to keep on denying self, when all nature cries out for an easier path. The gusty winds of temptation, or the arid plains of monotony, or the oppressive nights of loneliness, which are known only too well by missionaries and preachers (and by many lay Christians as well), make sustained self-discipline very difficult at times. Many a pastor has struggled with a desire to resign, when his deepest soul knew that God wanted him to keep on. Many a single Christian has fought the impulse to marry hastily and unwisely, realizing in his sane moments that he would be getting out of divine order. At such times one needs desperately the power and guidance of the indwelling Holy Spirit.

Admittedly there have been some fine exhibitions of sustained discipline when the motivation was not divine but quite human. Jacob submitted to the galling yoke of Laban for fourteen years, sustained by his love for Rachel. A modern example is the woman who conquered diabetes by weighing scrupulously every mouthful of food for two years until she was pronounced well. She was sustained by her intense desire to live without insulin. A few have stopped the use of tobacco on doctor's orders. But the day-by-day life of the Christian, not for two years, but for life, may impose perpetual disciplines on a much deeper level than these. The dynamic is not a desire "to save one's skin," but the love of God poured into the heart by the Holy Spirit.

4. That calls for one more statement defining the nature of sanctification as a foundation for discipline. This possibly is the deepest fact of all: holiness is needed to *purify one's motives* in seeking a disciplined life. Without Christian motives the discipline cannot be Christian. Which brings us back to Paul, "They do it to obtain a corruptible crown; but we an incorruptible." The sanctified person disciplines himself, not to save his body, but to save his soul; "lest I should be a castaway," Paul put it. Deeper yet—*lest by my becoming a castaway I should dishonor God.* One does not have to search Paul's mind far without discovering this underlying passion. Even in wanting to save his soul he was first and last seeking the glory of Christ. Thus the motivation for discipline becomes healthy when the believer is filled with the Spirit, and holiness by faith becomes, not the goal of discipline, but the foundation.

Do the Holy Still Need Discipline?

But if holiness has been reached, why the continued discipline? Cannot it now be laid aside as the scaffolding is removed after the building is finished? Is it not inconsistent to profess purity of heart and then admit the continued need for discipline?

Not at all, as we shall see presently. But first, let us concede that much unwholesome discipline will drop off when one finds perfect rest. Extreme and unnatural self-discipline is often but the flagellation of a restless, hungry heart, trying to conquer sin. Persons so afflicted often live a life of strain: they are overscrupulous and petty; prudish to the point of morbidity; easily shocked and quick to criticize others; afraid to laugh lest they be guilty of levity. This may be an unconscious attempt to compensate for some hidden sin, or hold at bay some beast of lust or hatred; or possibly it is an attempt to starve sin to death by making sure it gets nothing to feed upon. This is heroic and not to be despised, though it is to be pitied, for there is a better way. When by confession, brokenness, and cleansing such a person comes into full and happy adjustment he can relax, breathe freely, act naturally, and be a normal human being. The strait jacket is not needed when moral sanity has been reached.

But if there is grave danger that self-restraint may so "go to seed" as to lead to a character stalemate, there is also grave danger that a newly emancipated soul, rejoicing in his wonderful freedom, may suppose that discipline can now be dispensed with altogether. If there is no sin in the self, why the need for self-restraint? If the springs of life are love, why are taps needed to control their flow? If the aim is right, why muzzle the gun? In answer we can say that discipline in the sanctified life is not needed to muzzle the gun, but to hold the aim steady. It is not needed to shut off the flow of love from the purified springs of the heart, but to protect them from fresh contamination. But more than that, it is needed to *direct* the flow where it will do the most good and thus prevent the springs from overflowing aimlessly in every direction. Paul used a different figure but his meaning was the same: "I do not run aimlessly, I do not box as one beating the air" (I Cor. 9: 26, R.S.V.).

1. So then let us get down to plain prosaic truths. We can say *first* that discipline is needed even though one has been sanctified wholly because orderliness is an aid in *protecting the devotional life.* Some think that by practicing hard things they will strengthen their will power and thus fortify themselves against the onslaught

of temptation. There is some value in such will-training, but as a fortification against yielding in the hour of temptation it is greatly overrated. If the soul is starved, moral resistance will be weak, no matter what gymnastics have been imposed upon body and mind. Athletes at the peak of training are by no means examples of superior moral resistance. But the man of prayer is fortified. It is "by the Spirit that we put to death the deeds of the body," not by our strict regime. It is by the grace of God that the will is turned into steel, not by exercises. And the Spirit imparts His power through a deep and faithful prayer life. "Now unto him that is able to keep you from falling," said Jude. But our part is: "But ye, beloved, building up yourselves on your most holy faith, praying in the Holy Ghost, keep yourselves . . ." (vv. 20-21).

Therefore we must exercise some measure of discipline in order to see to it that our souls are at least as well cared for as our bodies. Regular devotional habits will pay large dividends. Haphazardness will starve spiritual life into anemia, and a starved soul is a poor spiritual risk in any circumstances.

2. *Secondly,* continued discipline is needed to keep the *body in its place.* Though it is "by the Spirit" that we put to death the deeds of the body, yet *we are still the ones* that do it. The power is given by the Spirit but the action is ours. Discipline is not the scaffolding: discipline is the building. It is the daily life in which the physical is kept subservient to the spiritual. Entire sanctification is not a fairy existence in which we are now exempt from such requirements; it is the equipage by which we now can meet such requirements.

After all, what is holy living anyway? It is devoted living, true; but it is also glorifying God in our bodies, which is another way of saying, using the body in harmony with God's will. As long as the body is clamorous in its very nature, just that long must one's authority be constantly asserted over it. "Killing the deeds of the body," "keeping under" the body, and maintaining the consecration of the body as a "living sacrifice" are life-long requirements. Such maintenance *is* disciplined living, in its primary sense. Specific aids to this end in the form of rules and schedules and prohibitions constitute discipline in a secondary sense, and may be helpful to a greater or less extent. But the one absolutely indispensable aid is the Holy Spirit. He does not dispense with disciplined living; He ushers us into it and helps us to acquire skill in maintaining and perfecting it.

3. In the *third* place, discipline is a proper facet of the holy life because without it the believer will not reach *maximum efficiency* in the Lord's service. Of itself the baptism of the Holy Spirit gives neither a trained mind nor trained hands. The holiest soul may be ignorant, awkward, and blundering. He may be haphazard and at loose ends. He may have no trade, skill, art, or profession. *But not for long.* If he is truly holy, in the Christian sense, he will not be content with begging; he will not exclaim as did the Indian fakir when asked why he didn't go to work, "Work? Why, I can't work—I am a holy man!" No, his inner renovation in pardon and purity will at once bring meaning and purpose into life, and inspire a hearty will to fulfill that meaning and achieve that purpose. Therefore he will immediately begin tying together the loose ends of his personality and bringing all his ransomed powers under tribute.

If there is a buried talent somewhere, it will be dug out and unwrapped. One woman had almost asphyxiated her musical ability by her worldliness. For seven years she had neither sung nor touched the piano. But when she was converted and sanctified she was encouraged by her pastor to attempt a resuscitation job. It wasn't easy. It meant digging into precious savings to buy a piano. It meant costly piano and voice lessons. It meant long hours of practice, month in and month out. It meant the sacrifice of many personal pleasures. It meant reorganizing everything. In short it meant *discipline*. But she became exceptionally useful as church pianist, and then as music instructor in her church Bible college. The grace of inner holiness gave her the impulse and dynamic for that sort of thing, but it was the subsequent grueling discipline that equipped her with sufficient knowledge and skill for the particular task. If a person is totally without ambition, holiness will give him some. But that ambition will never be realized, even when it is within the range of one's natural endowment, unless its possessor disciplines himself through the training, sacrifice, restrictions, inconvenience, and concentrated application which its realization may demand.

4. And what about *imposed* discipline, via rules and regulations of church, home, school? Surely the need for all that is dissolved in the purifying of one's heart! But this is not the case, and for a similar reason. Holiness purifies the heart but does not instantly mature the head. John Wesley insisted, "Much love does not mean much light." And Peter admonishes us to supply our zeal with knowledge. That takes time. In the meanwhile the zeal of youth may have to be subordinate to the knowledge of age.

In Christian colleges, for instance, young people with good hearts may need the restraint of rules and guidance of deans as much as anyone. They may be holy, but have incredibly poor judgment. A man will not necessarily exercise common sense in practical situations just because he is motivated by perfect love. In some situations the common sense may have to be exercised for him. Because a student at college may have good general intentions doesn't mean that he will always know when to come in at night, or how to conduct himself toward his girl friend or act in specific social situations, or how best to plan his curriculum or handle his time—without some instructions and perhaps a few rules. If the guidance is lacking, Satan may prey upon his inexperience and trip him into disastrous mistakes.

One student was deeply spiritual. His life and spirit were Christlike, and he sincerely desired to make good in his studies for the Lord's sake. But he was a disorganized dreamer. Only the whip of authority saved him from complete failure in his exams, by insisting that certain things be done at certain times and in a certain way. By temperament he was a law unto himself. Drastic measures were necessary to prevent him from becoming a useless saint. He had to learn to gear into life, not meditate forever in blissful freewheeling.

We may be ever so fit for heaven, but we are not there yet; and it is a pity to thwart our usefulness by being misfits on earth. God can use individualists, to be sure, but only when and if that individuality is tempered by some measure of practical adaptability. Therefore the student, even though holy, still needs schedules and regimes and requirements imposed upon him—possibly even some reprimands, penalties, and *F*'s. Out of it he will come forth as tempered steel. Many of us can say with the Psalmist: "Thou hast caused men [teachers, deans, pastors, committees, superintendents] to ride over our heads; we went through fire and through water: but thou broughtest us out into a wealthy place" (66:12).

CHAPTER FIVE

The Case for Imposed Discipline

Self-discipline is not only the ideal but the goal of all who work with children and youth. Self-reliance, self-control, and dependability are recognized everywhere as essential character traits for maturity and usefulness. But the best method for helping the growing person achieve these traits is a burning question.

A few would insist on no regimentation of youth whatsoever. Since character can be developed only from within, they reason, the individual should be left completely untrammeled and uncoerced. They would not exactly recommend a Topsy-like life ("I just grow'd"), nor quite agree that it is a case of tossing a child into the water as the best means of its learning to swim; for they would desire that the child be given instruction (when wanted) and even advice (when requested); and certainly they would advocate utilizing to the full the gentle but powerful influences of worthy example and environment. But to resort to the use of compulsion—no, never! In their view, surrounding the child or youth with daily demonstrations of disciplined adulthood is quite sufficient; indeed it is all that can effectively be done without stifling the inner development. The child must choose daily in absolute freedom. He will probably choose to emulate the character of his immediate adult associates, if in his view they are admirable and worthy of emulation. But if free choice is restricted by imposed discipline, the inner growth will be short-circuited.

In this view, imposed discipline, instead of issuing in mature self-control, simply creates the need for its own perpetuation. It is thus seen as a psychological drug, which so conditions the personality that it becomes indispensable. The use of the rod in the home, instead of so adjusting the character to law that the policeman will be unnecessary later on, merely conditions the character to the rod so that the person knows no other language, and the policeman will later on be not less indispensable but more so. The wine of force given for medicinal purposes produces not a well man, as is intended, but an alcoholic.

If this theory is applied practically, it means that the small child must be allowed to express itself naturally. Guidance should be given by example, suggestion, and the redirection of attention (in case Johnny is about to knock the pretty china off the mantel with a stick). Tantrums should be ignored; slapping at Mother should not be punished; the child should simply be shown something interesting so that it will forget its rage.

Years later, when in college, Johnny should not be hemmed in and sewed up by rules and regulations right and left, for this will dwarf his unfolding personality. He should be allowed rather to take the subjects he chooses, date as he pleases, go and come when and as he thinks best; for only then will he properly "find himself," and learn to restrain and balance and organize his life from *within*. If this view is correct, we should naturally expect that the homes with the least forcible restraint (assuming that example is found) should produce the sanest teen-agers, and the colleges with the fewest rules should produce the highest type of disciplined citizenry.

At the opposite pole are the rigid disciplinarians. In their view the rod should be within easy reach at all ages of minority. The lives of children and youths should be organized, directed, regimented from the cradle to marriage. Decisions are made for them; their sole duty is obedience.

The Current Awakening

The probability is that there are values in both viewpoints, and that either view collapses with the weight of its disvalues when carried to extremes. And in practice few actually would advocate total application of either theory. The trend however is away from the free-domestic vogue of the last few years to the frank admission that the absence of restraints is not producing better citizens, and that some blending of liberty and law must be applied at all ages. Highways must have boundaries as well as vistas. Freedom to roam the country must not be a freedom to climb fences and tread down vegetable patches. Responsible parents see this, and are coming to see also that some way must be found to help children see it too, *and see it at a very early age.*

Symptomatic of this trend is a shift of emphasis by the famous baby specialist Dr. Benjamin Spock. The revised 1958 edition of *Baby and Child Care* gives much more attention to the necessity of discipline than did the first edition published in 1946. This represents a deliberate attempt by Dr. Spock to offset a widespread tendency to carry the "flexibility" in child rearing, which he advocated in the first edition, too far. Parents had misinterpreted him to mean that (in his own words) "the baby should be allowed to make the decisions about how much of the day he was to be carried in his mother's arms. Often the same parents at a later stage thought they should permit their children to be inconsiderate and uncooperative, even rude." Writing about his aims in the new edition he explains: "When I saw the way the wind was blowing between 1946 and 1957 in overpermissiveness, I added, enlarged, and made more emphatic, material on parents' rights and children's need for control."

Here is another straw in the wind. When asked recently on the "American Forum of the Air" whether he believed our current education system was too easy, Dr. Hurst R. Anderson, president of the American Uni-

versity, replied, "I think we are soft, yes, I really do . . .
we are raising a generation of spoiled youngsters." Later
he expressed the view that, although modern methods of
child rearing and education could be traced to John
Dewey, the extreme laissez-faire doctrine, by which
Mother and everyone else allow Johnny to do as he
pleases without discipline, is a misinterpretation of
Dewey. Dr. Anderson concluded: "It is the problem of
American education, and the problem of the American
home to find the middle position between the two extremes, which is neither total discipline nor total freedom
and . . . I think we have been too far to the left in the
direction of too much freedom, and not enough discipline . . ."

Some have shied away from firm, old-fashioned discipline for fear of creating a personality vacuum, and
thus preparing the way for communism more easily to
commandeer the will. J. Edgar Hoover has reminded us
that under communism the individual "becomes an auto-
matic responder, not an original thinker." To forestall
such spinelessness, modern parents and educators right-
fully encourage individualism, love of freedom, independent action. Recently a mother whose fifteen-month-old
son was loudly protesting being dressed in the morning
explained, "He has a will of his own." A God-given piece
of equipment surely!—and his best protection against
future tyrants. No one wants that "will of his own"
destroyed. And so, to prevent its destruction, too often
mothers and fathers and all and sundry get out of the
way and let the little will run riot.

What Kind of Strength Do We Want?

But the fallacy is in supposing that such anarchy in
childhood and youth actually develops the character into
that kind of strength which is most apt to resist the
tyrant's yoke. Vigorous self-assertion, *of itself*, when
developed out of harmony with other facets of character,

can be nothing but a social cancer, which is the instrument of death, not life. For is not cancer the lawless development of a lot of little cells with "a will of their own"? Then when they have had their fling they do not protect and preserve the body which allowed them their freedom but kill it.

That kind of misdirected and perverted strength of will is the very thing that communism wants. It can exploit that sort of "individuality" most admirably, for such independence can quite readily bite the hand that has fed it, sever tender family ties, trample on Mother's tears and Father's pleas, disregard social mores, and despise the simple virtues of true democracy—honesty, integrity, respect for property and private opinion.

What must never be forgotten is that the kind of strength which is the surest defense against communism or any other sociological disease is far more than mere strength of will. Along with the self-assertion in the child and youth must be developed a sense of Christian values and balance. There must come the ability to think of others, their feelings and rights. There must be respect for property. There must be clear ideas of justice and fair play. There must be realization of the dignity of toil. A high regard for ideals and standards and laws must be woven into the very warp and woof of the soul. A generous-hearted optimism, love of people and God, a fine sense of social responsibility, an appreciation of common decency, an intense regard for human life, a capacity for warm loyalty and heroic self-sacrifice—these are qualities of character which are inherently antiseptic to all those ideological vampires which can only fatten on deceit, suspicion, and cruelty.

This balance is not going to be achieved by parents bowing to that "will of his own," and smirkingly boasting about it in the child's presence, and allowing him to go on unrestrained. That mother who as a guest in another home allowed her little four-year-old son to gouge holes in the leather seats of six new chairs while the hostess was out preparing tea probably thought she would warp his creative instincts if she laid violent hands on him. But the hostess when she saw the depredation could have put violent hands on him with a clear conscience. And if someone doesn't soon, the law will by and by, and the vandal grown up will glory in his strong will behind gray walls. In all justice, of course, the mother should be put in with him. It isn't fair for parents to prepare their children for jail and then let them go alone.

This suggests another reason why lack of vigorous imposed discipline does not produce that kind of strength which is a bulwark against communism. It is that humoring the child who has a "will of his own" does not result in even a strong will of the right sort. Allowing a child to do as he desires, to cry over nothing, to eat what he wants, to throw on the floor what displeases "His Majesty," to go into a tantrum when obstructed, to slap at Mother and kick at Father, while everyone chuckles, thinking that he is delightfully cute, will strengthen not only his self-will but his selfishness and his self-indulgence. This will bring his so-called strong will into bondage to his appetites. He is being conditioned to want what he wants when he wants it, without any capacity for deferment or denial. The resulting character will be not really strong at all but pathetically weak.

An unyielded will can never be strong in the best sense. It may be strong to defy, to destroy, to lash out at whatever stands in its way. But it is not strong to adjust to life's realities, to create beauty out of ugliness, to achieve over obstacles, to control self when frustrated, to work patiently and perseveringly in the face of difficulties.

And it is so often overlooked that such unintelligent "strength" is the first to succumb to the siren song of religious or political totalitarianism. Only provide these craven beings, whose "souls" are all body, a crust of bread and they come running. Cater to their appetites and their earthiness, promise them an abundance of things, and they will quickly barter their liberties, and bow in blind brute loyalty—which, incidentally, is the only kind of loyalty of which they are capable. The folly and gravity of selling their birthright for a mess of pottage is beyond their comprehension; the idea simply doesn't register. To reprove them for exchanging the values of the spirit for the values of the sod is futile, for they know nothing of spiritual values. They will not sacrifice their bread for freedom to think, to speak, to worship, but they will unhesitatingly sell their freedom to think, speak, and worship for bread. If such is the end result of parental pampering, then it is high time that parents alter their tactics and begin voting for democracy with the rod as well as with the ballot.

Civilizing with the Rod

And the rod won't hurt their budding personalities. It will prove not only an external stimulus but an internal tonic. One lad·after a sound whipping and after the tears were dried and reconciliation achieved said with a glow of gladness on his face, "I feel like I've had a bath on the inside." The whipping proved a sound investment in youthful character.

Firm discipline will not destroy a child's capacity to have a "will of his own" when he grows up and knows how to use it. We can conquer a child's will without breaking his spirit. That mother who said of her toddling son, "He has a will of his own," went right on dressing him in spite of his protests. And her four other children have known the gentle but firm and determined rule of both father and mother, with the occasional smacks and penalties involved, with the rewarding consequence that friends are always glad to invite the whole family when visiting time comes. Such high courage in contrast with the prevailing reluctance to include "those children" is more eloquent than words.

In another family are ten children—every one a credit to home and country. When a visitor took only *two* of them shopping, and bought some new clothes for only those *two*, a neighbor girl said to one of the left-out eight, "I'll bet you kids will kick up a fuss for being left out." "Oh, no, we won't," was the cheerful reply. "If we did we'd get a tanning where we sit down." On the contrary they had learned to give as well as take, and rejoice in the good fortune of each other. Without doubt they will make better citizens than the kind who would have kicked up a fuss, and their capacity for strong, independent action will not be warped either. A far cry from the parents who never dare take anything to their three children unless they purchase three just exactly alike!

A teen-ager greatly desired a position as a receptionist in a doctor's office. But the doctor thought she was too young. Finally he consented for her to help out for a week. The result was an amazed doctor, and a permanent job. Expressing his pleasure to the mother the doctor said; "What amazes me is to find such quick response and reliability in a girl so young. All I need is to tell her a thing once, and she does it promptly and efficiently."

Later that mother confided to me that she had never had to speak crossly or speak twice; from tiny girlhood the lass had moved quickly and pleasantly when a clear command was given. When pressed for an explanation she ventured: "Well, when she was just beginning to walk and talk, she one day spilled the entire box of scripture promise cards on the floor. I told her to pick them up and put them back in the box. In childish defiance, her little lip stuck out, she said, 'No!' But I quietly kept her there until finally she began slowly picking them up, one by one. I stood by without giving any assistance until every one was back in the box. She never said no to me again." Could there be a connection between that mother's firmness *then* and the girl's prompt obedience as a receptionist? I believe there is. And the submissiveness thus achieved did not stunt her, for *now* she possesses quite sufficient initiative and self-reliance in her new job. Neither did such "cruelty" impair the relationship between mother and daughter, for today their understanding comradeship is fine and beautiful.

Pampering Does Not Feed Love

The sober truth is, as many brokenhearted parents have discovered too late, that humored and coddled children do not love their parents more, but less. Their self-love is fed until it chokes out every noble impulse. Even their natural affection atrophies, and callousness takes over. They become incapable of real pity or sympathy, that fine sensibility to the heartthrob of another. A mother or father can slave and it doesn't evoke even a grunt of thanks. The parents can be breaking their hearts in sorrow and anxiety, and almost to collapse through overwork and strain, and such children *never see it*. If their attention is called to it, they are too heartless in their self-centeredness to care.

A mother arose very early every morning in order to have sufficient time to prepare seven different breakfasts for her husband, son, and five daughters, all of whom had personal tastes which must be pleased. The son and father were off to work first; then when the five feminine meals were ready, the harried mother would call her daughters, who were still lounging in bed. Years passed. The old mother, now a widow, found it necessary to live with her children, all of them married. But they didn't want her. Bickering over whose turn it was next, they passed her from one to the other. Finally they rationalized their consciences into putting her into an old people's home, where she was left to vegetate, with an occasional hurried visit. She didn't live long. It was claimed that she died of a broken heart. She had devoted herself unstintingly to her children because she had so pathetically wanted to be loved and appreciated. But unlimited pampering was the wrong method, as it dried up the springs of gratitude, and stanched the flow of natural affection. Notwithstanding, it would have been very hard, back there when her children were small, to have convinced her that her "kindness" was in reality the greatest cruelty both to herself and to her family.

It would appear that imposed discipline is more than justified. It is the salt in child training and youth directions without which the character putrefies before it ever reaches maturity. Even when, through counteracting religious influences, complete spoilage is avoided, and the undisciplined youth endeavors to lead a Christian life, he faces almost insurmountable personal weaknesses and handicaps, which make mature adjustment as an adult very difficult. Such a person does not appreciate the childhood freedom from restraint; rather he almost invariably chides his parents and wishes he had been better disciplined!

The young person who already has built-in habits of regularity and obedience certainly has a head start for effective and efficient living. The undisciplined youth, disjointed and at loose ends, may finally catch up, but it will only be by dint of much prayer and long, painful struggle.

The Scales Are Already Tipped

This is probably the logical place to point out that the assumption that example and indirect guidance are sufficient fails to take into account the sin principle. Children's natures are not placidly neutral; they are born with a bias. There is already a twist toward self-centeredness and lawlessness which will not right itself under the benign rays of Christian environment, but will feed on kindness, turn liberty into license, and grow alarmingly with the years, if not rigorously curbed by firm rule from the cradle onwards. Such curbing, while not able to extirpate the twist, will at least bring it clearly to light; it will also make adjustments to the restraints of an adult society much easier, to say nothing of the greater ease in submitting to the rule of God, at first partially, and then with that full submission which enables God to correct the nature at its base.

A large measure of self-control can be inculcated, which while it admittedly falls short of holiness, is nevertheless better than nothing. The measure of self-control in the world is exactly the measure of its safety as a decent place to live. Without some self-control in human character, life would be a frightful nightmare—as it evidently was before the Flood, and is even today in some areas. The greater the self-control (control of sex, of anger, of impulses, of speech), the greater the safety and happiness of any given community. But inasmuch as self-control is not natural nor easy (due to inbred sin), when is it going to be acquired? It should be acquired in early childhood. If self-control is not taught by parents, it will have to be taught by others later on. And if the school, or the police, or the army, have to teach it, the process will be much more painful and the success much more doubtful. Then let the parents do it!

In an editorial in the *Saturday Evening Post*,[1] Dr. Harry A. Snyder of the Pennsylvania Bureau of Correction discussed an analysis of 486 juvenile offenders in comparison with a comparable group of normal high school students. After pointing out the similarities and differences, he concluded, "Absence of home discipline could be the factor which transcends differences of class, economic status, and race." He goes on to say, "If there is any remedy for disrespect for the law, dearth of moral

[1]December 3, 1960.

values, and absence of religious guidance, it appears that the family circle must assume the primary responsibility."

Such views should be taken very seriously by Christian parents. But it is a challenge which will be met only by strong purpose and unwavering consistency. Weak parents who are undisciplined themselves will succumb to infantile and juvenile rule. It is much easier to give in when Johnny and Mary storm than to take them firmly in hand. But if such parents could once see the disastrous consequences which await both themselves and their children, and that their weakness is a crime against society and a sin against God, they would turn to their task with unflagging resolution.

The Fear Motive

But the task will be infinitely easier if well begun the first four years of a child's life. *Then* the habits of regularity and obedience need to be formed—but that is too early for matters to be left to Johnny's infantile judgment! Sanctions must be enforced. Obviously at this age the fear motive must be brought into play. Fear seems an unworthy motivation to many, but it is not really so. It is far better for a child to learn self-control through fear than not to learn it at all. At least the child knows what is expected, and that painful consequences follow wrongdoing; and there could be no more basic lesson than this.

As Dr. Philip S. Clapp points out, it does not necessarily demand extreme physical measures to accomplish the desired end, if the training is begun soon enough. He says, "It will not require cruel punishment, possibly nothing more painful than a slap on the hand, to teach a small youngster that No means No and that he'd better cooperate with family rules and regulations. The secret is in having him learn as early in the game as he is able to demand his own way just because he wants it, that he cannot have it at the expense of others' rights and well-being."

When a three-year-old feels impelled to strike his sister but restrains his hand out of fear of the stinging consequence, he has learned a lesson in self-control. There is plenty of time later for love and intelligence to replace the warm posterior as the motivation. But the ability to control one's impulse to physical action has already been achieved. And that ability is the foundation of all worthwhile character. *Mature* self-restraint is a yielding to *sanctions within,* imposed by the conscience and judgment; certainly that is the goal. But the first step toward that goal is learning to yield to sanctions *without.*

The fact that one's character may never reach full maturity and that the fear motive may never be outgrown, is no sufficient reason for failing to lay at least this much of a foundation. Think of the social chaos if the fear motive for decent behavior were totally removed! Fear of hell, of disease, of jail, of financial loss, or fear of public opinion, may be less than ideal motivations, but they are better than no curbs at all. Better to restrain one's lust for speed out of regard for the tough police officer patrolling this stretch than to kill everyone in two cars because one scorns the "fear motive"!

The Philadelphia Youth Study Center has this slogan: "The difference between the delinquent and the non-delinquent youth is the pause between the temptation and the act." Commenting on this the *New Zealand Herald* in a leading editorial says: "The young criminal, vandal, ruffian or pervert, in other words, obeys the impulse of the moment, seeks selfish advantage, despises authority and rule, and cares for no will but his own. The self-discipline which inhibits such action must come from within, but that is impossible unless it is first inculcated from without." The same editorial quotes a prominent British penal official as using a stronger word:

Discipline is developed from within "when it is enforced from without." Enforcement is at times and at some stages in the child's development a necessary supplement to persuasion. Without it his moral and social education may prove fatally defective.

Disciplining Adults

It has often been conceded that he who cannot control himself is not fit to control others. It is just as true that he who cannot follow is not worthy to lead, and he who cannot obey orders is not qualified to give them. Teaching obedience, instead of short-circuiting self-control and developing only moronic automatons, is the surest way known to produce self-reliance and self-control. Athletic coaches know this. The army and navy know it. Officers are trained by rigid regimentation and often humiliating subordination. At least during war-time when quick, sure results are imperative!

During World War II a documentary film showed a military officer in the making. Almost every hour was budgeted, church attendance enforced, visitors limited. One young cadet was shown cheerfully bounding up the steps two at a time when an officer standing nearby commanded him to halt. The cadet saluted, grinning. The officer sternly commanded: "Wipe that grin off your face!" The youngster moved his hand across his face, now sobered, in a wiping motion. "Now throw it down and tramp on it!" came the further order. The cadet obediently went through a throwing motion, then stamped on "the grin," still keeping a straight face. "Now go back down the steps and come up one at a time like an officer!" He obeyed. Was this just horseplay? No, one of the world's greatest nations, in desperate war, was trying to make a leader. His superiors knew he must have perfect self-control. They had no fear that such abject obedience would stultify his personality or maim his capacity for initiative.

The ability to administer discipline as skillfully and accurately as the surgeon wields the scalpel is one of the universal marks of the great leader. The world-renowned sacred musician Robert Harkness once had in his choir a soloist of rare talent, who phoned him one morning and announced bluntly that she was resigning. He replied instantly, "Your resignation is accepted."

There was a surprised sputter on the other end.

"You mean that?" she gasped.

"Indeed I do," affirmed Mr. Harkness. "You joined the choir of your own free will and you can resign if that is your choice—but you may be sure the committee will write you a letter expressing their appreciation of your fine work."

"But may I come to see you and explain first?" she pleaded.

When she came she reminded him—though not quite so sure of herself now—"But, Mr. Harkness, I have not been asked to sing a solo for a whole month!"

"If that is your reason," said Mr. Harkness firmly, "you have done the right thing in resigning, for you obviously have been singing, not to the glory of God, but for the glory of self, and there is no room in our choir for such singers. You cannot come back unless you change, and surrender fully to the Lord. Go home and think about it for a month."

At the end of three weeks she came to him: "Mr. Harkness, I have decided to surrender fully to God and seek only His glory. May I come back?"

"Certainly," he replied, "but the seat in the front row which was formerly yours has now been assigned to someone else. You come to rehearsal this Friday night and we will find a seat for you in the back."

After the rehearsal the woman said to him: "I am willing to sit any place hereafter; the humblest place is more than I deserve." Warmly the great musician said, "That's what I like to hear! And to prove I believe you,

I want you to sing a solo next Sunday night." She did;
but though the voice was the same, the singer was trans-
formed. The masterful touch of unexpected discipline
had brought her to a spiritual awakening.

For many years now we have been panicky about
any kind of church discipline for fear of losing people.
But we have lost them anyway. I wonder how many
might have been saved if a little loving but firm discipline
had been applied at the right time in the right way.

PART TWO

The Path to Discipline in Christian Living

CHAPTER SIX

How to Become a Disciplined Person

In this chapter no attempt is made to be novel or original, and certainly not exhaustive, or even particularly scientific. The suggestions are simplicity itself. There is nothing expensive or complicated; and there is nothing beyond the understanding and ability of any person young or old of average intelligence. And I will drop all formality and speak directly to the reader.

No Short Cuts!

1. Begin by reading the entire book through, including the Introduction, if you have not already done so. Some of you will spot the title of this chapter while scanning the *Contents* and, recognizing that becoming a disciplined person is the goal, will suppose that to read only this chapter will be sufficient. Such an attempt may be symptomatic of your need of discipline.

The undisciplined person is forever seeking ways to avoid the arduous grind of solid work and to arrive quickly at his goal by short cuts. He would have butter without having to churn the cream. He would have the broad vistas without having to climb the hill. We face such persons constantly. They want a quick and easy way to the knowledge of the Bible, to become musicians, to learn to preach, to be well informed, to obtain a degree. But there is no quick and easy way. A willingness to undertake the labor involved in becoming disciplined is the first step in achieving our desires; for this reason the suggestions in this chapter will be of very little value excepting as they are seen and applied in the light of the basic principles which have been presented in the previous pages.

If you need to reinforce your motivation, then ponder soberly and honestly the end result of drifting through life as an undisciplined person. Think of the disappointment that you will be to yourself, to God, and to your dearest loved ones, by failing to be the man or the woman that you must be to accomplish anything worthwhile in life, simply through sheer slothfulness in taking firm hold of yourself and refashioning your character.

Read Luke 9:62.

Where to Begin

2. Having determined to become a disciplined person, begin with the simple things. Hang up your clothes. Make your bed promptly and neatly, wash out the bathtub or washbasin after yourself, put your shoes in their place, clean the tools you use and put them where they belong—and where either yourself or another can find them next time. Don't scorn these trifles as being irrelevant to a disciplined character; they are the very essence of it. For they indicate just that extra touch of foresight, of carefulness, and of thoughtfulness which makes the difference between slovenliness and refinement. A disciplined person seeks to avoid making unnecessary work for others. He also is concerned about the aftermath, not just a good showing now. It is said that the coeds of a certain college always stepped out of their rooms chic and elegant, every hair and eyelash in its place; but the rooms they stepped out of were shambles. Their fund of orderliness was so meager that it was exhausted on their backs.

Read Song of Sol. 2:15.

Training the Body

3. Practice a relaxed but steady control of bodily movements. Constant fidgeting, shifting, and scratching, not only is a sign of "nerves" but feeds the condition.

A vicious circle is thus set up. Defects in this area are not always the expression of basic physical or nervous ailments but often just plain bad habit. Break these bad habits.

Begin with your hands. Learn to keep them still. Get the feel of holding them loose at your side, and see if it doesn't increase your sense of poise. Don't allow your hands to tyrannize you by constant restless motion, such as tapping, or cracking knuckles. Shake hands firmly and warmly; then let go courteously and positively. Don't cling. And keep your hands off the opposite sex.

Then begin working on your posture. Shuffling feet and habitual slouch give people the vague, uneasy feeling that your mind shuffles and slouches too. An outward alertness in stance and carriage not only conveys a better impression, but tends to create the feeling of life and sparkle within yourself. Don't be stiff and starchy, forever standing on your dignity; nobody likes a prig. But stand tall, sit tall, walk tall, and then even your laugh will have a wholesome "tallness" about it.

Then watch your eyes. Practice looking at the person to whom you are speaking or listening. President Case of Boston University avoids the habit of looking past his conversationalist, or gazing around, as if he were bored, but looks at the person in front of him in complete attentiveness, as if no one else mattered at that moment. You must avoid embarrassing people by staring at them, of course; don't fasten your eyes intently on their pupils as if you were trying to hypnotize them; nothing is more disconcerting than a solemn, fixed stare. But still, keep your eyes in warm friendliness in teamwork with your voice and mind. Avoid the nervous shiftiness, the vacant look, the restless wandering, which advertise a lack of concentration and interest—in fact, an undisciplined mind. And when in a public gathering, train yourself to keep your eyes on the speaker. To gaze around at people

or down at your feet, or to thumb idly through the hymnal, is rude and discourteous.
Read Eccles. 5:1.

Whip the Hard Ones

4. Tackle difficult tasks promptly and energetically. Do first the things you would rather do last. If you are a pastor, let the hardest call lead the list for the day. If a student, get at the boring assignment at once, with the determination not only to conquer it but to like it. And this practice can be combined with another, equally important: Complete what is begun. Other duties may interrupt, but force yourself back to the task. It is said that Coleridge could have been as great a writer as Shakespeare, but instead his literary career was littered with scraps of unfinished masterpieces, begun in high spirits but not carried through.

It is true that at times we begin projects which prove impossible to complete. At other times we awaken to the grim fact that our undertaking *ought not* to be carried out; its commencement was a bit of bad judgment and to pursue it would be added bad judgment. Then quietly back out, as gracefully as possible. But beware lest numerous starts and few finishings become both a habit and the badge of your undisciplined character.

As a young student in college, Wallace White found himself responsible for a tedious and complicated plumbing job. Somehow the administration had learned that he was a plumber by trade, and in their great emergency called on him for help. Glibly he agreed. But when he discovered how long it would take, and saw that the gigantic task would seriously affect his strength and studies, he felt like "throwing in the towel." Almost he went to the office with the words: "Look, I would rather you get someone else for this job." But knowing that quitting had been his weakness in his preconversion days, and determined to make himself fit for the Master's use,

he resolutely said to himself: I will not quit. It took six months to do the job. But at the end there was not only repaired gas service throughout twenty buildings but a repaired character in a future missionary. Later, en route to the wild highlands of New Guinea, he told us humbly: "I felt that experience was a test, sort of a turning point in my life. I sensed that if I failed then I would fail later in some more serious situation." And he was probably right.
Read Prov. 22:29.

Cultivate Punctuality

5. Make yourself be punctual. Tardiness is another bad habit which needs to be broken, and which any intelligent person, alert to life's obligations, can break. When students glibly cast off their tardiness by the cliché, "Better late than never," Professor Mae Bower of California fame would invariably retort, "Better never late." Then she would remind her students that "trifles make perfection, but perfection is no trifle." And punctuality is one of the "trifles," though verily a huge one.

But the habit of being on time will never be acquired unless (1) you are convinced that Christian courtesy demands it—which brings the issue into the realm of ethics; (2) you plan ahead, so that you know without guessing where you need to be and exactly when; (3) you allow yourself a generous margin of time. Some sort of diary or daily reminder must be kept, into which all appointments can be entered, as well as relevant data concerning bus or train timetables, payment schedules, insurance due dates, and of course all regular church and departmental activities. But even such a diary is of no value unless it is consulted frequently, and the week's program planned accordingly. And even this will not make us efficient, prompt persons unless we eliminate the superfluous, undertake a little less, and then start soon enough to arrive (or be prepared for others to arrive) without breathless flurry and jangled nerves. Look ahead, and start early. These are the two wings of the life that soars.

The man who always lives by split-second timing is apt to die of ulcers before he is fifty. Instead of living up to par, with time and nervous energy to spare, he is scurrying around in a daily "rat race." John Wesley said, "I am always in haste but never in a hurry." He meant that, though he had no time for idleness, he allowed himself sufficient time for his undertakings to carry them through calmly and punctually. The man who thus lives with a margin may have less native ability than the "worry wart," but he seems to have more. He gives the impression of reserve, of quiet strength; others sense that here is a man who knows where he is going and how to get there. And he arrives on time, without fussing and fuming.

Read Rom. 12:11.

Girding Up the Mind

6. "Gird up the loins of your mind," is the Biblical injunction. Gather up your mind, organize the loose ends, draw into service your wandering thoughts, just as an Oriental of Peter's day would quickly gather up his "loose robes with a girdle when in a hurry or starting on a journey" (A. T. Robertson).[1] This is no day for disorganized minds to be flapping loosely in the breezes of daily impulse.

There are many ways of honing your mind into razor efficiency. One is to try concentrating on a problem in pure thought without visual or social aids. This is not easy. We are so accustomed to having our stream of thought directed and guided by pictures, the printed page, and lively conversation that, on our own, our minds flop like jelly, or skip here and there like children. The

[1] *Word Pictures in the Greek New Testament,* VI, 87.

problem or idea we are trying to catch and hold plays
hide-and-seek. It is nebulous, evasive. But keep at it.
Detach yourself from mental props, sit quietly, and *think*.
Stay with it until the problem begins to focus. Ask
yourself questions, and proceed to answer. What is the
main issue? What is the heart of the matter? When
Peter spoke of mind he meant, says Robertson, the understanding, the "faculty of seeing through a thing." This is
the capacity for clarity. You must think until muddled-
ness is gone. When the matter is clear to yourself you
can then make it clear to other people.

In this seeking to gird up the loins of your mind,
practice thinking in sentences. The very effort to organize thought into grammatical form tends to bring orderliness into the thinking. Logic takes hold. Self-criticism,
correction, revision begin to perform their magic. As you
improve the sentences, the thought itself takes on clarity.
Then you begin to see through the thing.

Furthermore, in thus seeking to discipline your mind,
it is wise to undertake systematic courses of instruction.
A minimum level of education will be required by law.
But the youth who is alert to life and wants to be more
than a part-time hatrack will not be content with the
minimum. For consecration to God carries with it the
obligation to excel, not in competition with others, but in
competition with oneself. God's work demands trained
minds. You have no right to be mediocre if you are
capable of something better. Therefore undertake a program of learning. Enrollment in a school even for night
classes or correspondence work will force you to organize
your time and overcome obstacles; if you persevere you
will emerge not only with an enlarged fund of knowledge
but with the added strength of character and agility of
mind which accrue as by-products of the discipline. And
this is the case where the by-products are more important
than the main product.

The same dividends can be earned both for physical and mental discipline by learning one or two skills which require painstaking, nerve-racking concentration, to achieve perfect co-ordination of brain and hand. Knitting, possibly. Or piano, or organ. Or touch typing, a skill which can be of such incalculable value to almost anyone. Other things being equal, the person who makes himself draw a violin bow back and forth until the screech becomes a silvery tone; or sit at a piano teaching his awkward fingers to obey the messages given by the brain, which at the same instant is trying to make sense out of the funny-looking marks on the music score; or sit at the typewriter with an aching back fixing the taut mind on a mental picture of the keys, until finally after many months the fingers fly in quick response to the lightning of thought, and the pain gives way to pleasure and the strain becomes conquest—such a person on the whole is apt to be more disciplined and resourceful than the one who has never taken the trouble to learn any sort of skill.

Read I Pet. 1:13.

Exploiting the Unexpected

7. Learn to turn to good advantage the unscheduled twist of events which throws your well-laid plans into confusion. Since even a methodical and careful man cannot always avoid such upsets, he must achieve that maturity which knows how to absorb and exploit them. The finest self-discipline is seen, not in rigidity, but in resiliency. Here are some simple rules:

(1) See that fretting is folly. It will change nothing, excepting as it changes a sunny mood into a sour one. Fretting is the reaction of the small man, whose imagination is stunted, whose stock of ideas is exhausted, and whose life is self-centered. The big man refuses to waste nervous energy in fruitless sputtering.

(2) Thank God for His hidden providence. Claim

the "all things" of Rom. 8:28. Recognize quite humbly that what seems to you at the moment nothing but human blundering may be the gentle steering of God. Someone has observed that not only the steps of a good man are ordered by the Lord but his *stops*. That Christian worker in England during the war who felt it imperative to catch a certain bus but missed it due to delays beyond his control, and had to wait an hour for the next one, was tempted to fret—until the bus he did take overtook the one he missed, now twisted and battered by a fallen bomb, its passengers corpses. Rarely however is such a divine providence so quickly vindicated. Generally the merciful design behind a permitted delay is not revealed at once, and this is well, since the puzzles of providence are good for faith.

(3) Ask God to show you how to turn your frustration into His fulfillment. Look for the human need which you probably would have missed in your bustling efficiency. A professor friend found himself marooned on a waiting room chair one afternoon, without a book to read or a pad on which to write. Sensing that several hours would probably be lost thus, and thinking of the important work that was waiting, he felt himself begin to tighten up inside. Then deliberately and prayerfully he relaxed and looked around. Opposite him was a harried and worried mother with a sick child in her arms and another fretting at her feet, tugging at her skirt and demanding attention. It was not long until the university professor won the little one's confidence and had her on his lap, where he kept her happily occupied until the very grateful mother was out of the doctor's office and ready to go home. And his own heart was strangely warmed. The afternoon had not been wasted—it had been invested. Too often the would-be disciplined person provides only for the *ideal*; when unideal developments engulf him he is thrown off balance. We must learn to

take the raw material of the *real* and transmute it into service.
Read Rom. 8:28.

Love Your Critic

8. Cultivate an attitude of sincere gratitude for all correction. Thank the person who points out a grammatical error, for he is handing you a piece of material for the disciplined character you are building. A preacher of my acquaintance had unconsciously picked up a habit of using a certain phrase until it was annoying. But when told about it, such was his control that he did not repeat it a single time thereafter.

Petulance or supersensitiveness when corrected shows immaturity. A recent magazine cartoon depicted a young secretary on the floor in a tantrum, tears flowing profusely, fists pounding the carpet. Her middle-aged boss benignly looked down at her saying, "Miss Davis, you must learn to take correction." And so must *you*.

To accept either correction or instruction graciously is difficult at times, especially when we doubt the justice of it, or more especially when we question the other's qualifications to instruct us. But Adam Clarke said: "Be willing to learn from the lowliest. Remember it was the gaggling of geese that saved Rome." The well-known holiness expositor Joseph H. Smith found himself an object of curiosity many years ago as he sat reading his Bible on the ferry en route from Oakland to San Francisco, where he was to be the chief speaker in a holiness convention. Many other preachers were on the same ferry, keenly anxious to hear this highly recommended advocate of the second blessing. But another colorful representative was there too, a quaint eccentric, who felt it his duty to identify himself with these "peculiar" people by wearing a little tin hat with a scripture motto on it. Presently Dr. Smith was aware that the eccentric had quietly sat down beside him. Fearing that the skeptical onlookers would come to associate the holiness movement with freakishness, he was sorely tempted to ignore him. But suddenly he came in his reading to the verse: "Be courteous to all." Instantly he held out his hand exclaiming,

"Good morning, brother!"

His visitor replied, "Pardon me, Brother Smith, I hesitated to disturb your reading. But when in prayer for you the Lord showed me that you suffered with a certain ailment, and that I was to tell you how to cure it. I know the cure works, for I had the same trouble."

Then to Evangelist Smith's amazement he named a malady with which he had struggled for years without finding any successful treatment. Later he followed his advice and was entirely relieved. He thanked God that that morning on the ferry he had not snubbed the quaint man with the little tin hat; and for the Lord's rebuke in the pithy sentence, "Be courteous to all."

Prov. 15:32.

Self-restraint

9. Assiduously practice the manly art of exercising self-restraint in at least these three areas (where precipitate effervescence is the universal human tendency):

(1) *Curiosity.* It is the curious person who learns, discovers, and invents, it is true, but in social niceties one can be what ultra-frank youngsters call a "stickybeak." Sometimes it is wise to refrain from prying too indelicately into other people's affairs.

(2) *Prejudice.* This actually is nothing but prejudging. It is the opinion or conclusion which has been formed on insufficient evidence. It can be most viciously unfair to others and in time will disclose your own immaturity and imbalance. To suspend judgment at times, and to refuse to be stampeded into rash action by agitators, are twin evidences of a disciplined character. This leads to the third:

(3) *Dogmatism.* Certainly the true Christian is basically a dogmatist. He affirms some things positively and consistently. But the habit of being dogmatic about everything is a perversion of the Christian temper. Some cannot state opinion without being opinionated. Some can never express themselves except in a bombastic and uncharitable manner that says: This is the last word. There is no other side. Anyone who can't see this is a numbskull. Such grand assurance is highly amusing in teen-agers, but distressing in adults, as it reveals arrested development. Don't misunderstand! I would not have you become insipid neutralists who drift with the wind, always tentatively hovering and never settling. There are times when it is refreshing to find someone who is unafraid, when the issue is important, to speak out vigorously in a fine display of dogmatic, fist-pounding affirmation. But there are other times when Christian restraint not only has opinions but allows them. In curiosity, prejudice, and dogmatism, therefore, "let your moderation be known unto all men."

Read Prov. 18:13.

Conquer Gluttony!

10. We are together coming now to one of the most difficult lessons of all in the school of discipline: the conquest of the appetite. I refer to the appetite for food. There should be abstinence from poisons and temperance with food. But temperance is sometimes more difficult than abstinence. Eating is not a sin but gluttony is. The person who is habitually self-indulgent in eating and drinking, without regard to health or need, almost as if he lived to eat rather than ate to live, is very apt to be weak and exposed in other phases of his life. Flabbiness in one area of character tends to loosen the whole.

This is a difficult problem which calls for a good stock of common sense as well as iron will. Without common sense we are apt to be faddists. Without strong purpose we will be gourmands. On the one hand is the peril of morbid bondage to a supersensitive conscience; on the other hand there is the peril of being in bondage to the stomach. Speaking of food Paul said: "All things are lawful for me, but I will not be brought under the power of any." Anyone under the power of food has little claim to the high rating of disciplined character.

It is not necessary to be unsociable in one's eating habits. One should eat heartily and with enjoyment. But we should know what is good for us and how much, and have the self-control to stop. The best exercise, it has been said, is "the push-ups"—up from the table. Details should not be determined by popular books on diet but by consulting a competent physician.

The importance of achieving temperance in eating can hardly be overemphasized. Its crucial place as a sort of key to control in other areas has already been mentioned. But general health, efficiency, and longevity are affected too, and these are heavy with the issue of God's glory. Excessive overweight almost always means underproduction in the work of God. When therefore overweight is the result of overeating, we will be held accountable for every surplus pound. Fat kills, but it is our duty to live, that we may declare the wonderful works of God. Let overwork, or unavoidable exposure, or persecution and martyrdom, shorten our lives in the service of the King, and we can die with honor. But if life is shortened by self-indulgence—what then will we say when we stand in the presence of our defrauded Master?

Read I Cor. 9:25-27.

Learn to Respect Time Tags

11. Many of life's most important joys, privileges, and responsibilities have a time tag on them. They

belong to certain days, or to the end of a set span of years, or to a certain level of maturity. To grab them too soon is to spoil them. Yet if our typical modern character has any weakness more outstanding than another it is this inability to wait. "I want what I want when I want it" is the prevailing approach to life.

Commenting on the failure of so many young couples to await proper marriage for the consummation of their love, Dr. Dwight Small says: "Too many young people are nothing but spoiled children who must have immediate satisfaction for all their urges." He calls this an "immature attitude," and how right he is! But how did they get that way? By being allowed to eat as children when they chose, instead of being required to wait for mealtime. By being permitted to "jump the gun" on their birthday and on Christmas by opening their presents before the day arrived. By being permitted to drive a car before they were legally eligible to do so. And so life became a pattern of cheating the calendar, of seizing privileges and pleasures before they were entitled to them. Since such young people are less and less capable of accepting delays with gracefulness and self-control, they are not apt to do so when caught in the tide of life's strongest urge during courtship.

If you would become a disciplined person, you must decide that, no matter what your previous pattern has been, you will never again try to tear off proper time tags. If you are a young person, don't open those packages until Christmas. Let four years of high school and four years of college be four years, respectively. Let courtship and marriage await their proper time and process. You will never be sorry for waiting for joys to come in God's way and time.

And let major responsibilities come when God sees you are ready. Do not try to force providence. A very young minister avidly desired a certain pastorate. The district superintendent said to him: "I wouldn't be fair to you if I put you there." In his naive ardor the youth thought he wasn't being fair *not* to put him there. But he lived to be everlastingly grateful to that superintendent. In another instance a young man felt clearly called to a certain field of service twenty years before he got there. Was God's calendar mixed up? No, it took God twenty years to get *him* ready. The processes of maturation cannot be hurried, and only disastrous consequences will accrue when we try. We do not help God by opening a rosebud—we simply spoil the blossom! Many young men have had to taste the bitter frustration of failure because they were thrust into responsibilities for which they were not ready. Therefore if you would be a disciplined person you must learn to respect life's time tags. *Read Eccles. 3:1.*

Welcome the Yokes of Life

12. But while waiting for major responsibilities to come in God's time, you can best prepare for them by cultivating a *sense of responsibility*. This always goes with maturity; without it maturity is impossible. Let your attention be outward, toward your family, that church committee of which you are a member, tonight's missionary meeting. Realize that these groups need you. You owe to them your loyalty, your presence, your cooperation. Don't be like a giddy, irresponsible adolescent who can gaily let others do all the work while he enjoys himself. Don't be a butterfly who promises to take part in the youth meeting but fails to show up because at the last moment the impulse came to flit somewhere else.

One with a sense of responsibility is one who *feels responsible*. This sense was well expressed by Walter Rowe Courtenay: "I personally feel that I owe a double duty to life: a solemn duty to my ancestors, and a pressing duty to my descendants." It was expressed even better by the hymn writer:

I would be true, for there are those who trust me.
I would be pure, for there are those who care.
I would be strong, for there is much to suffer.
I would be brave, for there is much to dare.[2]

You can check your progress toward a mature sense of responsibility by asking yourself these questions:

—Am I faithful to keep appointments?

—Can I be depended on to fulfill tasks assigned to me?

—Am I quick to take hold and help when a job is to be done or do I find it easy to slip quietly away?

—Do I accept responsibility for my decisions and mistakes, and do I share the responsibility for the decisions and mistakes of my group, or do I tend to shift the blame to others?

—Am I careful about financial obligations, or do I require the prodding of duns?

You can doubtless think of many other questions which are equally good indicators of the maturity of *your* sense of responsibility.

Read Lam. 3:27.

Cultivate Prayer Patterns

13. A systematic prayer pattern is a prime essential in our quest, for two reasons. I will mention the lesser one first. The very effort to achieve regularity in prayer habits is in itself disciplinary. There is no better preventative against sloth. Even grace before meals has its disciplinary value. The simple act of sitting quietly at the table, not touching food even when ravenously hungry until grace has been said, is a counteractant to the tyrannizing pull of appetite. In the same manner does

[2]Howard Arnold Walter.

regular family worship impart to the participants an element of strength, not only because of the benefits of worship, but because of the planning and restraint required in the act of getting together at one time in one place, each one laying aside his own activities and subordinating his own independence. The "family that prays together stays together," not only because they pray, but because the discipline demanded by praying *together* will make them steadier and stronger all along the line.

But the second and deeper reason is that we want above all that the disciplined character we develop shall be truly and thoroughly *Christian*. We desire to become disciplined persons, not for the glory of self, but for the glory of God. But our motives will be thus Christian only as a vital prayer relationship with God enables His grace to undergird and crown our every effort. On our own we may achieve a facade of poise and strength, but only as we pray will the outward show be authenticated by matching reality and genuineness within. For in the end we want to be, not just self-made disciplined persons, but God-made. Only then will our disciplined character be truly Christian.

Read I Pet. 4:7.

A Philosophy of Discipleship

14. The Holy Spirit said through Paul: "Endure hardness as a good soldier of Jesus Christ." In these days there is not much hardness to endure. This is true at least of physical discomforts. (Even spiritually, when the prestige of religion, including holiness denominations, is at an all-time high, we know little of facing up to the stinging rebuff of opposition.) As a consequence our young people, who have taken luxuries for granted until they have seemed like necessities, who have lived in comfortable homes, driven the best cars, enjoyed high school popularity, had money to spend, and attended college where they were accustomed to lavish meals and

pleasant rooms and the amenities of plush student union buildings, have too often reached adulthood so conditioned to soft living that they have been totally unfit for any sphere of service which demanded ruggedness and simplicity, such as the foreign field, or even the small home mission pastorate. As Vance Havner says, "When we feather the nest too well the eaglets do not fly."

There is only one antidote to the softening tendencies of our many blessings: a rugged philosophy of discipleship, grounded in a bedrock experience of holiness. The scriptural cue for this philosophy and experience, of course, is the mandate of Jesus: "If any man will come after me, let him deny himself, and take up his cross, and follow me." A full exposition of self-denial and cross-bearing as conditions of discipleship cannot be attempted here. I want to major on three ideas which are more directly relevant to our immediate quest. Now back to *you.*

(1) *You* must be so thoroughly sanctified, so thoroughly dead to self and the world, so thoroughly spiritual in your viewpoints and standards of value, that you will not be inordinately attached to material things—*anything:* fine furniture, lovely dishes, a certain climate, proximity to your kin, a three-bedroom house.

"A tent or a cottage, why should I care?"—that's pretty tough meat for the natural man to swallow. For of course in the natural you *do* care—you prefer a cottage to a tent. But you care for something else far more—the will of God. You would like to have some things, but you can be happy without them if you can only know that you are in the center of the will of God. In fact you know down in your heart of hearts that you would prefer a tent to a cottage if the cottage could be had only at the cost of the will of God. What am I saying? Simply this: When Jesus said, "A man's life consisteth not in the abundance of the things which he possesseth," He was expressing truth which must be real to you, not just a threadbare platitude to which you render lip service.[3]

(2) Then this philosophy of discipleship must include a clear-eyed perception of the perils of ease and prosperity, and the necessity of compensating by some deliberate bits of self-imposed ruggedness. It is at this point, as well as others, that fasting has real value. Esther Carson Winans, heroic missionary to the Aguaruna Indians in Peru, while in Pasadena College deliberately practiced eating unpalatable food to train herself for the days when eating it might be a necessity. She evidently believed that a little self-imposed hardness in college might help her to endure hardness later on when it wasn't self-imposed!

Anything which helps us avoid softness, and counteracts the enervating effects of prosperity, is all to the good. And it's the simple things that make the difference. We must refuse to let a bit of weariness or disinclination keep us from prayer meeting. We must refuse to allow our faithfulness in church duties to be dictated by circumstances, convenience, or feelings. When life does not buffet us, we must buffet ourselves. When God prospers

[3]There is nothing wrong with a house and garage full of gadgets provided we can give an affirmative answer to three questions: (1) Will their acquisition be too costly? I don't mean monetary cost; that may be the least of their price. But if health is undermined, the soul is starved, the church is neglected, the finances jeopardized, and the family disorganized in the mad, desperate effort to pay for them, then the game is not worth the candle. "Better is an handful with quietness, than both the hands full with travail and vexation of spirit" (Eccles. 4:6). (2) Will there be cultural and spiritual gains which will make the family more closely knit, and the individuals in the family finer persons? (As for instance might be true of a record player—provided it played the right records.) (3) Is there any net gain in time and energy which accrues to the kingdom of God? If our "surplus" time is absorbed in operating and maintaining the gadgets, or if the added leisure is used simply in multiplying our own selfish interests, then the resultant benefit to others is precisely nil. In that case we are not investors but spendthrifts.

us we must then of all times refuse to be easy on ourselves; rather we should be more daringly faithful than ever, and make sure that there is enough Spartan rigor built into our lives to maintain always the spirit and readiness of a true soldier.

(3) Then it is imperative that our philosophy of discipleship embrace as axiomatic the principle that Christlikeness is the goal of life, not happiness. The current philosophy around us is that all is well if only people are happy. The great aim of education, science, and government is to give the most temporal happiness to the most people. And even as Christians we have been infected by the spirit of the age so that we bargain with God for happiness. If cross-bearing is *Christ's* condition of discipleship, happiness is *ours*. But it cannot be so. Discipleship cannot be thus compromised. It must be self-denial and cross-bearing whether happiness is always the immediate and apparent consequence or not.

If our philosophy of discipleship is thoroughly Christian we will see that our choices and decisions and vocations are not to be determined by a feverish pursuit of personal happiness. Furthermore, our success or failure as Christians or as Christian workers cannot be measured by whether or not we are at the moment happy. Paul was not always happy, nor was Luther, nor Wesley. But discipleship for them was not happiness; it was faithfulness and usefulness.

This philosophy will hold missionaries steady when they are lonely and homesick. This will keep pastors from resigning and seeking greener pastures when problems become complicated and the burdens are almost too heavy to be borne. This will keep husbands and wives true to each other when incompatibilities seem to make ideal happiness beyond their reach. This will keep students grinding toward the goal of God's call whether they *like* studying or not. This will keep laymen faithfully tithing and working and worshiping even when caught by contrary winds of adversity or emotional depression.

This will also help young people face up to God's call for their lives. Elizabeth Cole, the intrepid and radiant missionary to the lepers in South Africa, honored with the M.B.E.[4] by the Queen of England, tells of her struggle as a young woman to give up the freedom of her wild Montana hills. She was a cowgirl, with "the most beautiful horse in the world." When God called her to train for medical missionary work, the very thought of being cooped in a city and in a hospital as a trainee was appalling. She felt suffocated. The typical vocational guidance expert would have counseled: "Never consider it! You are not cut out for such a life. *You wouldn't be happy doing that!*" Fortunately she didn't come under the thumb of such a helpful expert. She wasn't settling the business on the basis of happiness but on God's call. Ultimately, in her mature ministry in Africa, she found glorious happiness, far richer and deeper than she had ever known in her carefree days on the hills of Montana; but she couldn't foresee such happiness when she first confronted God's plan.

And what is true of happiness in general is true of fun and pleasure in particular. Let us once for all drum the truth into our heads that there can be no room in the Christian life for hedonism. Fun will not be chased as the goal of life. Play will be an occasional restorative, not the perpetual pursuit. There will be many pleasures along the way which will be enjoyed gratefully; but the Christian must never become preoccupied with the frantic quest for pleasure for its own sake. Even excessively numerous hobbies and holidays can choke out our vocational effectiveness.

[4]Member of the Order of the British Empire.

For the Christian life is serious and challenging and demanding. It is not seen as either a glorified picnic or a dress parade, but a field of battle. Our Captain is the world's Redeemer, who "pleased not himself." Let us be His disciples. Without this spirit of earnestness and commitment, this passion for the cause of the Kingdom, our efforts to become disciplined persons will be abortive and vain. But with this spirit our discipline will find its Christian purpose and fulfillment.

We can summarize then by saying that he who is in possession of a Christian philosophy of discipleship will demonstrate it by

—a passion for improvement, for Jesus' sake;

—a sense of stewardship toward life, for Jesus' sake;

—a readiness for sacrifice or service, for Jesus' sake;

—and, as he matures in *The Disciplined Life*, an increasing capacity for steady application to the task in hand, *for Jesus' sake.*

Read Phil. 2:5-11.

CHAPTER I

Questions for Further Discussion

1. What are some of the positive values in sports? When does sports activity and interest become detrimental rather than helpful?

2. Which of the five dangers foreseen by Theodore Roosevelt (p. 18) most accurately describe our current society?

3. Can you think of anyone among your acquaintances whose professional career failed to reach expectations because of character weaknesses? Or anyone whose physical or mental breakdown could be related to undisciplined living?

4. Is there danger that a young Christian might exhibit sufficient discipline to reach the top in his chosen field, yet miss God's will, and be motivated by pride and ambition? What might this suggest?

5. Which is the more satisfying reward of disciplined living, vocational achievement or the knowledge that our example is having a strengthening and stabilizing effect on others?

CHAPTER II

Questions for Further Discussion

1. Can a person who has a tendency to dislike discipline become a mature person in spite of this trait? How?

2. In what area of life are immature Christians (in either spiritual experience or age) most apt to be relatively undisciplined? What are the dangers of "accepting" this weakness as something they can't help?

3. Can character maturity be prevented by unwise reading? by unwise viewing and radio listening? What would you classify as "unwise"?

4. Can you see any relationship between disciplined appetites, emotions, moods, speech, etc., and the fruit of the Spirit (Gal. 5: 22-23) ? What might this suggest about the Spirit-filled life?

5. What is the most common and at the same time most devastating moral failure in modern society? Can this be traced to lack of discipline in some one particular area? Which?

6. Will unusually strong discipline in one area make up for lack of discipline in another? Does this teach us anything about the nature of true maturity?

CHAPTER III

Questions for Further Discussion

1. Let us suppose a young person, either by providence or by special calling, is denied some of "God's good gifts," contrary to his natural desires. He accepts the special form of discipline required of him, rather than disobey God. Can you think of any special peril which may beset him in regard to his attitudes?

2. Some unchristian cults exact of their adherents a high level of discipline. (Black Muslims, for instance, eat one meal a day, avoid immorality, alcohol, tobacco, and give strict obedience.) In what sense can this constitute a peril to the devotee? Might it also become a peril to the observer? How?

3. Which is harder—to achieve an inflexible pattern of living or to achieve a disciplined flexibility?

4. Which is the greater peril to society—too much discipline or too little? Which extreme largely prevails in our day?

CHAPTER IV

Questions for Further Discussion

1. While discipline is not to be accepted in lieu of holiness, what must be said about the "brand" of holiness that is content to dispense with discipline altogether?

2. What must be said about the devotion of Christian students who allow non-Christians to outdistance them in disciplined application to their studies?

3. Is there a difference between a carnal (sinful) aversion to discipline which can be removed in entire sanctification and a temperamental dislike, which itself must be perpetually disciplined after sanctification? If so, try to pinpoint it.

4. Is it always easy for a sanctified Christian to accept imposed discipline from others? Is his capacity to absorb discipline graciously and wisely an index of his holiness only, or also an index of his maturity?

5. Can a Christian rebel against discipline, or flaunt the known standards and rules of his group (church, school, etc.), and remain spiritually genuine and vital?

CHAPTER V

Questions for Further Discussion

1. What are some of the more common faults observed in modern parents in the training of their children? What suggestions would you make toward improvement?

2. At what age is the "fear motive" most effective, and usually most necessary? Should this motive be exploited by frightening the child with lies, such as, "I'll call the police, and they will put you in jail"?

3. What qualities of mind and character are necessary in parents if they would be successful disciplinarians? Does this have any bearing on teen-age marriage?

4. What evidence have you observed that children and young people have a greater sense of security in an environment of reasonable discipline than in an environment without discipline?

5. Could you suggest any principles for determining the line between what (or when) parents should choose for their child and when the child should be allowed to choose for himself?

6. What form of discipline is best for teen-agers? How much liberty should they have?

7. Comment on the last paragraph of the chapter.

CHAPTER VI

Questions for Further Discussion

1. Moderns tend to avoid both silence and solitude. What bearing, if any, would a larger amount of each have on becoming a disciplined person?

2. Try suggesting other scriptures (possibly better ones) appropriate for each division of this chapter.

3. Would this chapter have been strengthened by a section on the handling of money? Is extravagance related to disciplined living? How? What about the well-to-do who can afford to be extravagant? Are the character implications less serious for them? What suggestions would you include if you were writing such a section?

4. What suggestions in this chapter are most appropriate to the special problems of youth? of adults?

5. What is the relative importance of a sound philosophy of discipleship to the rest of the chapter—or even the entire book? Defend your answer.